Shepherding Peace:

Pastoral Letters from an Inclusive Church; The Christian Demand for Justice

By

Presiding Bishop George R. Lucey, FCM
(American National Catholic Church - ANCC)

Dedication

These writings are dedicated to the glory of God,

and to all the People of God who seek, in every age,

to discover the meaning of divine love

revealed in the Church and its sacraments.

Acknowledgments

I wish to express my gratitude to the clergy, religious, and faithful of the **American National Catholic Church**, whose prayer, generosity, and witness to Christ's love have inspired these reflections.

To my brother and sister pastors who serve with compassion and joy; to the parishes that live the Gospel at the margins; and to all who continue to believe that the Church can be a home of mercy — I offer my thanks and my blessing.

These pages were born from our shared journey of faith, from the stories and struggles of the People of God who embody the compassion of Jesus in daily life. May the same Spirit who has guided our Church continue to renew and strengthen us in the service of God's kingdom.

George R. Lucey
Bishop, American National Catholic Church

Apostolic Blessing

Through the intercession of the Blessed Virgin Mary,

the apostles Peter and Paul, and all the saints,

may Almighty God bless you,

the Father †, and the Son, and the Holy Spirit.

Amen

Table of Contents

Introduction and Purpose

This volume gathers the American National Catholic Church's theological, pastoral, and ecclesial reflections on Catholic Social Teaching. These materials began not as an academic project, but as pastoral letters written to speak directly to the People of God in the ANCC and in the Church Catholic. Their primary purpose was to ensure that our Church added her voice to the social issues affecting the faithful—offering guidance that was pastorally sensitive, theologically grounded, and rooted in the Gospel's call to justice, dignity, and communion.

These letters were crafted in response to the real moral and social concerns shaping the lives of our communities. They sought to accompany the faithful with compassion where there was suffering, clarity where confusion was growing, and courage where silence would have failed the demands of charity. In this way, they expressed the ANCC's commitment to engage the world in the spirit of the Second Vatican Council: attentive to the signs of the times, grounded in conscience, and faithful to the Church's social mission.

Over time, and at the suggestion of one of our clergy, it became clear that these letters could serve an additional purpose. Their theological coherence, pastoral tone, and conciliar grounding made them a natural foundation for a resource to support those preparing for ordained ministry. What began as direct pastoral outreach to the faithful has grown into a structured tool for formation—helping seminarians and all who serve the Church understand how the ANCC receives, interprets, and lives Catholic Social Teaching today.

For this reason, the volume now serves a dual purpose: first, to preserve and present the pastoral letters in their original intent as guidance for the People of God; and second, to offer them as a resource for the women and men preparing for ordained ministry in the American National Catholic Church.

To support this expanded purpose, the collection includes:

- The pastoral letters themselves, presented as primary theological and pastoral texts

- A Vatican II–shaped hermeneutical key to guide interpretation

- Formal theological introductions aligned with conciliar documents

- Academic tools such as discussion questions, a graduate-level syllabus, and MLA citations

- A concluding ecclesial statement articulating the ANCC's Catholic identity and credibility

Together, these materials reveal an understanding of Catholic identity grounded not in juridical recognition but in the lived commitments of the Church: apostolic faith, sacramental life, episcopal ministry, and a communion-oriented ecclesiology. Authority is exercised pastorally and collegially; conscience is honored as a genuine locus of moral truth; and Catholic Social Teaching is presented as an expression of Eucharistic communion rather than ideological advocacy.

For seminarians and all who seek to understand the ANCC's mission, this resource is both foundation and invitation. It presents a Catholic body shaped by the Council's vision of a Church engaged with the modern world, attentive to the cries of the poor, and committed to dialogue and doctrinal development. It offers a model of conciliar reception that is pastorally responsive, theologically coherent, and ecclesially grounded, an orientation essential for the ministry and service to which we are called.

Author's Preface

I write these pastoral letters not as final answers, but as faithful responses offered in particular moments of pain, hope, and moral urgency. They arose from prayer, listening, and a deep love for the People of God entrusted to my care. If they speak with clarity at times, it is because silence would have been a failure of charity; if they speak with tenderness at others, it is because the Gospel itself is tender.

My hope is that these letters will be read not only with the mind, but with the heart—within the larger communion of the Church, attentive to conscience, and open to the Spirit who continues to lead us into truth. May they serve, in some small way, to build peace as communion.

— George R. Lucey, FCM

Presiding Bishop

American National Catholic Church

Purpose and Scope

The pastoral letters of the American National Catholic Church (ANCC) are not isolated interventions reacting to passing events; taken together, they constitute a sustained theological witness. Rooted in Catholic doctrine, shaped decisively by the Second Vatican Council, and attentive to the lived realities of God's people, these letters express an ecclesial conscience formed at the intersection of Gospel fidelity and historical responsibility.

This introduction offers a theological framework for understanding the categorization of these letters, articulates why each group belongs within its respective conciliar lens, and reflects on how the ANCC embodies Catholic Social Teaching in a manner both faithful and prophetic.

At the heart of this collection lies a conviction articulated by Gaudium et Spes: that the joys and hopes, griefs and anxieties of the people of our time are also those of the followers of Christ. The ANCC's pastoral voice emerges from this same ecclesial responsibility—to interpret the signs of the times in the light of the Gospel while remaining grounded in the Church's living tradition.

Hermeneutical Key for This Volume

The pastoral letters gathered in this volume are to be read neither as isolated reactions nor as partisan interventions, but as acts of ecclesial discernment.^1 They arise from what the Second Vatican Council described as the Church's responsibility to "scrutinize the signs of the times and interpret them in the light of the Gospel" (*Gaudium et Spes*, §4). This hermeneutical key rests on the conviction that history itself is a theological locus—a privileged place where God continues to reveal, challenge, and console.

Within the American National Catholic Church, pastoral teaching is understood as a dialogical act. Scripture, tradition, lived human experience, and conscience are held together in prayerful tension.^2 This approach stands squarely within the Catholic tradition as received through Vatican II, while also acknowledging that doctrine develops in its expression as the Church deepens its understanding of the human person and the demands of justice.

Accordingly, each pastoral letter in this collection should be read as:

- Rooted in Catholic doctrine and the conciliar vision of the Church

- Addressed to concrete historical circumstances rather than abstractions

- Shaped by a sacramental worldview in which grace is encountered in human struggle

- Ordered toward communion, healing, and the common good

What follows are formal introductory essays for each theological category. These introductions are intended to precede each group of letters, offering the reader a theological lens through which to receive the texts that follow.

Statement on the American National Catholic Church as a Credible Jurisdiction of Catholicism

The materials submitted here, including the pastoral letters, theological introductions, conciliar framework, and academic apparatus, are offered as a comprehensive ecclesial statement concerning the Catholic identity and credibility of the American National Catholic Church (ANCC). Taken together, they demonstrate that the ANCC understands itself, and conducts its life and ministry, as authentically Catholic, conciliar in orientation, sacramental in practice, and pastorally responsible in governance.

Catholic Identity Rooted in the Second Vatican Council

The ANCC locates its Catholic identity squarely within the reception of the Second Vatican Council. Vatican II remains the decisive hermeneutical key by which the Church understands its relationship to tradition, authority, conscience, and the modern world (Second Vatican Council, *Gaudium et Spes* 4). The ANCC receives the Council not selectively or ideologically, but integrally—embracing its ecclesiology of communion (*Lumen Gentium* 1), its pastoral engagement with history (*Gaudium et Spes* 1), its commitment to religious freedom and conscience (*Dignitatis Humanae* 2), its liturgical vision (*Sacrosanctum Concilium* 14), and its mandate for ecumenical and interreligious dialogue (*Unitatis Redintegratio* 1; *Nostra Aetate* 2).

This reception places the ANCC firmly within the mainstream of postconciliar Catholic theology. The Church's self-understanding as the People of God, called to holiness and co-responsibility through baptism, is consistently reflected in its pastoral teaching, governance, and sacramental life (*Lumen Gentium* 9–12).

Apostolic Ministry and Pastoral Authority

The ANCC exercises episcopal ministry in continuity with the historic Catholic understanding of pastoral authority: authority ordered toward communion, service, and the building up of the Body of Christ (*Lumen Gentium* 18). The pastoral letters submitted here exemplify the traditional role of the bishop as teacher, sanctifier, and shepherd—addressing matters of faith, morals, and ecclesial life in response to concrete historical circumstances.

Pastoral authority within the ANCC is exercised collegially and pastorally rather than juridically alone. Teaching authority is understood not as coercive power, but as a responsibility to form conscience, articulate moral truth, and accompany the faithful in discernment, in keeping with the Council's vision of episcopal ministry (*Christus Dominus*11).

Fidelity to Catholic Doctrine and Development of Teaching

The ANCC affirms the central doctrines of the Catholic faith: the Trinitarian confession of God, the Incarnation, the sacramental economy, the centrality of the Eucharist, and the moral dignity of the human person (Catechism of the Catholic Church 232–267; 1691–1698). At the same time, it acknowledges—consistent with Catholic teaching—that doctrine develops in its expression as the Church reflects more deeply on the Gospel in changing historical contexts (*Dei Verbum* 8).

The pastoral letters demonstrate a method of doctrinal fidelity that is neither static nor relativistic. Moral teaching is articulated through conscience, pastoral accompaniment, and discernment, drawing on Scripture, tradition, reason, and lived experience, reflecting the Catholic moral tradition as renewed by Vatican II (*Gaudium et Spes* 16).

Catholic Social Teaching as Ecclesial Witness

Catholic Social Teaching is integral, not ancillary, to the ANCC's understanding of Catholic faith. The Church's sustained engagement with issues of justice, peace, human dignity, inclusion, and the common good reflects the Council's insistence that social responsibility flows directly from the Church's sacramental life (*Gaudium et Spes* 26).

The pastoral letters submitted here demonstrate that Catholic Social Teaching is not ideological advocacy but ecclesial witness. They embody a Catholicism that speaks prophetically while remaining pastorally grounded, consistent with the social magisterium from *Populorum Progressio* to *Fratelli Tutti* (Paul VI; Francis).

Sacramental Life and Ecclesial Communion

The ANCC's sacramental practice reflects a deeply Catholic understanding of grace, symbol, and community. The Eucharist is understood as the source and summit of ecclesial life, ordered toward healing, reconciliation, and mission (*Sacrosanctum Concilium* 10). Sacramental discipline is exercised pastorally, with an emphasis on participation, formation, and communion rather than exclusion, reflecting postconciliar sacramental theology (Chauvet).

This sacramental vision undergirds the Church's ecclesiology and moral teaching, affirming that the Church exists as a visible sign of God's reconciling love in the world (*Lumen Gentium* 1).

Ecclesial Credibility and Catholicity

Credibility in Catholicism is not established solely through juridical recognition, but through fidelity to the apostolic faith, sacramental life, pastoral governance, and communion-oriented ecclesiology (*Lumen Gentium* 8). The ANCC submits that it meets these criteria through its sustained reception of Vatican II, its episcopal ministry, its theological coherence, and its lived pastoral practice.

The materials presented here demonstrate that the ANCC is not a reactionary or sectarian body, but a Catholic jurisdiction committed to the ongoing work of conciliar reception. It understands itself as part of the broader Catholic tradition, bearing witness to a form of Catholic life that is faithful to doctrine, attentive to conscience, and responsive to the signs of the times (*Gaudium et Spes* 4).

Concluding Affirmation

In submitting these pastoral letters and theological materials, the American National Catholic Church affirms its identity as a credible jurisdiction of Catholicism. It offers this witness humbly, not in opposition to other Catholic bodies, but in fidelity to the Gospel and in service to the People of God. The ANCC stands within the living tradition of the Church Catholic—rooted in apostolic faith, nourished by the sacraments, guided by the Second Vatican Council, and committed to the work of justice, peace, and communion in the world.

Introduction – The Church at the Margins

The Church has always found its truest voice at the margins. It was at the edges of the empire, among the poor and the outcast, that Jesus first proclaimed the reign of God. It was among the overlooked and the weary that he called disciples, broke bread, healed wounds, and revealed the heart of divine compassion. The Church's mission has never been to defend its own importance but to embody that same love, a love that goes out, seeks, and welcomes.

In my ministry as bishop of the American National Catholic Church, I have come to see the margins not as places of failure but of revelation. It is there that the presence of Christ is most visible, not in triumph but in tenderness, not in dominance but in mercy. The ANCC was born from this conviction: that God's grace knows no boundary, that all are invited to the table, and that inclusion is not a modern concession but the very pattern of the Gospel.

Our Church stands as a witness that the Catholic faith is vast enough to hold the full diversity of God's people. We are Catholic not because we mirror Rome's structure, but because we share in the same sacramental life, the same apostolic hope, and the same universal call to holiness. We are a community of seekers and servants, striving to live the ancient faith with renewed compassion, integrity, and joy.

This book gathers pastoral letters and reflections written out of that ongoing work, the daily effort of guiding, teaching, and walking with the People of God. These writings are not abstract theology; they are born from encounter: from visiting communities devastated by storms, from standing beside victims of violence, from blessing the hands that serve at the altar and the hands that feed the hungry. Each letter carries a moment in time when the Gospel demanded to be spoken with clarity and love.

Catholic Social Teaching provides the structure for these reflections, but the heart of this book lies in the lived experience of our communities. The principles of human dignity, solidarity, and care for creation come alive not in policy statements but in faces and stories. They are the living theology of the Church that prays, serves, and loves in the name of Christ.

As your bishop, I have learned that teaching is not a matter of authority alone but of listening, listening to the Spirit who speaks through the faithful, through the cries of the poor, and through the hopes of those the world forgets. The Church's role is not to offer all the answers but to accompany, to discern, and to nurture the seeds of grace already growing in the hearts of God's people.

This is what I mean by peace as communion: a peace that comes not from uniformity but from relationship; not from the absence of tension but from the presence of love. The peace of Christ binds us together across difference and distance. It is the peace we celebrate in the Eucharist — where heaven touches earth, and strangers become one body. From that table, we are sent to build what we have received: a reconciled world, a Church that heals, a community of hope.

The sampling of writings in this volume is offered as a companion for that journey. They reflect the faith of a Church that is both ancient and new, deeply rooted in the Catholic tradition, yet open to the movement of the Spirit in our own age. They are written for anyone who seeks to live the Gospel fully: for clergy and laity, for the confident and the questioning, for all who hunger for a faith that embraces the whole of life.

My prayer is that these pages may serve as moments of grace, invitations to see the world through the lens of communion and to discover again that the heart of the Church still beats with compassion. May these reflections help us remember that peace is not a distant dream, but the shape of love made real.

George R. Lucey
Bishop, American National Catholic Church

Chapter I:
The Church in the Modern World (*Gaudium et Spes*)

Introduction to the Letters in This Category

The pastoral letters gathered under this heading reflect the Church's vocation to engage the world not from fear or withdrawal, but from compassionate presence and moral responsibility. *Gaudium et Spes* decisively situates the Church within human history, affirming that the suffering, injustice, and hope of the modern world are not external to the Church's mission but integral to it (§1). These letters arise from the conviction that silence in the face of injustice is itself a theological failure.

Addressing gun violence, racism, immigration, political responsibility, war, and environmental stewardship, these texts embody the Council's insistence that faith must be incarnated in concrete social realities. They do not offer technical policy prescriptions; rather, they seek to form consciences shaped by the Gospel and oriented toward the common good. In this sense, they function as pastoral applications of Catholic Social Teaching rather than ideological statements.

The inclusion of these letters together reflects a consistent theological posture: the Church must read contemporary events sacramentally, discerning where human dignity is violated and where the Spirit calls the faithful to conversion, solidarity, and action. Drawing on the trajectory from *Populorum Progressio* to *Fratelli Tutti*, these letters affirm that peace, justice, and human flourishing are inseparable from authentic Christian discipleship.

Readers are invited to approach these texts as expressions of a Church striving to be what Vatican II envisioned: a humble companion to humanity, a prophetic witness against structures of sin, and a bearer of hope grounded not in political outcomes but in the reign of God already breaking into history.

August 28, 2025

Feast of St. Augustine

Pastoral Letter on the Tragedy of Gun Violence

When Herod realized that he had been outwitted by the Magi, he was furious, and he gave orders to kill all the boys in Bethlehem and its vicinity who were two years old and under, in accordance with the time he had learned from the Magi. Then what was said through the prophet Jeremiah was fulfilled:

"A voice is heard in Ramah,
weeping and great mourning,
Rachel weeping for her children
and refusing to be comforted,
because they are no more."

— Matthew 2:16-18

My dear brothers and sisters in Christ,

On this Feast of St. Augustine, I find myself reflecting on his words about the ministry of bishop: "What I am for you terrifies me; what I am with you consoles me." As I write to you today, in the wake of yet another school shooting here in the United States, I take consolation in our faith lived together as the Body of Christ. And yet, I share with you a profound sorrow and righteous anger over the senseless gun violence that has claimed the lives of two young children and left many others injured.

We cannot look upon such tragedy and remain unmoved. These children, killed even as they prayed at Mass, are in the truest sense, the Church's newest martyrs. Their deaths expose once again the moral and spiritual crisis in which our nation finds itself — a crisis marked by political paralysis, by the idolatry of weapons, and by a refusal to recognize that the so-called "right" to own guns has been placed above the lives of our children.

As Christians, our baptismal vows call us to love God and neighbor. To take up arms against children, or to defend systems that perpetuate such slaughter, is the complete denial of that baptismal promise.

As American National Catholics, we have borne witness to the distortion of Christ's command to love. We have seen how His preferential option for the poor, the vulnerable, and the marginalized has been co-opted by movements that cloak themselves in the language of Christianity, yet preach a gospel of supremacy, exclusion, and fear. They proclaim a Christ who is unrecognizable to the Christian soul.

History continues to repeat itself when its lessons go unheeded. Hatred, violence, and indifference grow where love is silenced. But I believe we, as the ANCC, are called to be a clear and unwavering voice a visible sign of God's love in the world. We must work to end the rhetoric of division, to find common ground, and to welcome with compassion our immigrant sisters and brothers, our LGBTQIA+ siblings, and all those who have been radicalized by voices of hate echoing across our world.

On this feast, St. Augustine reminds us of the power of love to renew what sin destroys: "People are renewed by love. As sinful desire ages them, so love rejuvenates them." In another homily he exhorts us: "If we receive the Eucharist worthily, we become what we receive." As Catholics, we profess that the Eucharist is the source and summit of our lives — the Real Presence of Christ among us. That reality must take flesh in us. To receive the Eucharist is to become Christ's presence for the world: to be agents of justice, builders of peace, and bearers of love.

Today, in the shadow of yet another national tragedy, let us recommit ourselves to this mission. Let us embody Christ's love in our lives and work tirelessly for a society where children may grow in safety, where love is stronger than hate, and where peace is more powerful than violence.

May the God of peace strengthen us, may Christ's love guide us, and may the Spirit renew us in courage and hope.

In Christ's peace,

Most Rev. George R. Lucey, FCM
Presiding Bishop
The American National Catholic Church

July 4, 2025

Memorial of St. Elizabeth of Portugal

> *Woe to the shepherds who mislead and scatter the flock of my pasture, says the Lord. Therefore, thus says the Lord, the God of Israel, against the shepherds who shepherd my people: You have scattered my sheep and driven them away. You have not cared for them, but I will take care to punish your evil deeds.*

—Jer. 23:1-2

In the Name of the Father, and of the Son ✝, and of the Holy Spirit.

Grace and peace to you.

The American National Catholic Church joins its voice with those of the United States Conference of Catholic Bishops and other faith leaders in expressing deep concern over the passage of the misleadingly named Big Beautiful Bill. This legislation threatens to inflict the greatest harm on those who are most vulnerable and most in need of the support our government can—and should—provide. To deny such care in the interest of protecting the wealth of the few is not only a moral failing, but stands in direct contradiction to the teachings of Christ and the core values of human dignity and mutual respect found at the heart of our Catholic tradition.

As a faith community rooted in the radically inclusive love of Christ, the American National Catholic Church affirms our call to civic responsibility. We are mindful that the framers of our Constitution were deeply influenced by the idea that natural law, derived from God, endows all people with inherent rights—rights that uphold human dignity and foster a just and moral society in which all may flourish.

Guided by the Holy Spirit and grounded in the universal (catholic) teachings of Jesus Christ, the ANCC believes that government, like the Church, should serve the common good and uplift the many, not just the privileged few. As Gaudium et Spes, the Pastoral Constitution on the Church in the Modern World, reminds us:

> *"The political community exists for the common good, in which the community finds its full justification and meaning."*

It goes on to teach that:

> *"It is in full accord with human nature that juridical political structures should, with ever better success and without any discrimination, afford all their citizens the chance to participate freely and actively in establishing*

the constitutional bases of a political community, governing the state, determining the scope and purpose of various institutions, and choosing leaders."

On this Independence Day, as we celebrate our nation's founding and the Declaration that proclaimed liberty from an unjust monarch who saw his subjects only as means to enrich his treasury, we are reminded again of our Christian call to be a people who bind up the wounded, heal the sick, welcome the stranger, and bring home the lost.

We must also remain vigilant in rejecting the false prophets of our time—those who would twist the Gospel to deny Christ's preferential option for the poor; who seek to strip others of their dignity based on race, language, sexual orientation, or gender; and who foster policies that marginalize and demonize those who are different. These are not the values of Christ.

We know our voice is small—indeed, often a voice crying out in the wilderness—but we must be relentless in opposing the tide of greed and corruption that betrays the Gospel. We proclaim not the rule of empire or personal wealth, but the reign of the One True King, whose Kingdom is built on love, justice, and the common good.

In New York Harbor stands a statue bearing the name Liberty Enlightening the World. At its base are the words of Emma Lazarus:

"Give me your tired, your poor, your huddled masses yearning to breathe free."

This hope lives still—in the spirit of every American and in the heart of every immigrant who has come seeking a place where human dignity is honored and peace is possible. Yet today, that hope is darkened by the passage of a bill that betrays our deepest values and uses rhetoric meant to divide rather than unite.

As Christians, we are called to stand in the breach, to lift up the truth, and to remind one another of the mission entrusted to us by Christ. We serve the One King who came not to be served, but to serve—and to love us all.

✚ Amen

Most Rev. George R. Lucey, FCM

Presiding Bishop

February 8, 2025

Memorial of Saint Jerome Emiliani

I have been in contact with our clergy and families who have immigrated to our country and with members of the LGBTQI community. In light of their experiences, I invite you to join the American National Catholic Church in standing in solidarity with all who are affected by discriminatory policies, advocating for dignity, justice, and inclusion for all.

Most Rev. George R. Lucey
Presiding Bishop

Official Statement from the American National Catholic Church

The American National Catholic Church (ANCC) proclaims itself a sanctuary community, standing in unwavering solidarity with all our sisters and brothers, especially those who are marginalized, vulnerable, and in need of refuge. Rooted in the Gospel call to love our neighbor and guided by the principles of justice, compassion, and dignity for all, we commit ourselves to being a safe and welcoming home for all who seek belonging and peace.

As followers of Christ, we affirm the sacred worth of every person, regardless of nationality, immigration status, race, ethnicity, gender identity, sexual orientation, or socio-economic condition. We extend our hands and hearts in hospitality to our immigrant brothers and sisters, recognizing their inherent dignity and the many gifts they bring to our communities. We stand in steadfast support of our LGBTQI sisters and brothers, celebrating their God-given identities and embracing them fully within the life of the Church.

The ANCC rejects all forms of discrimination, oppression, and exclusion. We denounce any laws, policies, or actions that seek to divide, dehumanize, or marginalize individuals based on their identity or circumstances. In the spirit of the Good Samaritan, we pledge to be a voice for the voiceless, a place of refuge for the displaced, and a community of radical inclusion, where all are welcomed, loved, and affirmed.

We call upon our clergy, faithful, and all people of goodwill to join us in this sacred mission—to be instruments of peace, bearers of hope, and builders of a world where justice and mercy prevail. As a sanctuary community, the American National Catholic Church will continue to walk with those who seek safety, embrace those who long for acceptance, and advocate for the dignity and rights of all God's children.

> *"Come to me, all you who labor and are burdened, and I will give you rest."*
>
> *(Matthew 11:28)*

In Christ's Love and Service,
The American National Catholic Church

January 24, 2025

Memorial of St. Francis de Sales, Bishop and Doctor of the Church

> *"Do not fear, for I am with you; do not be afraid, for I am your God. I will strengthen you, I will help you, I will uphold you with my righteous right hand"* - *Isaiah 41:10*

In the Name of the Father and of the Son+, and of the Holy Spirit.

Dear Beloved Immigrant Priests and Faithful People of God in the American National Catholic Church,

Grace and peace to you in the name of our Lord Jesus Christ.

In these times of trial and uncertainty, we write to you with hearts full of gratitude and admiration for your courage, faith, and perseverance. The recent illegal ICE raids, marked by their cruelty and intent to intimidate, have shaken the peace of many communities. Yet, amid these challenges, your unwavering commitment to proclaiming the all-inclusive message of the Gospel shines as a beacon of hope and love for all.

Your dedication to serving God's people—often in the face of fear and injustice—is a testament to the strength of your faith and the boundless love you embody. You remind us all of Jesus words: "Blessed are those who are persecuted for righteousness sake, for theirs is the kingdom of heaven" (Matthew 5:10). Your ministry and witness inspire the entire American National Catholic Church and call us to deeper solidarity with one another.

Please know that you are not alone. We, as the wider Church, stand firmly and lovingly by your side. Your struggles are our struggles, and your safety and well-being are of utmost importance to us. We are committed to doing everything within our power to provide support, protection, and advocacy for you and those you serve.

If there are specific ways we can assist—be it through legal support, community outreach, or creating safe spaces—please do not hesitate to reach out. Our love for you and our commitment to justice compel us to act. Together, as one body in Christ, we will continue to proclaim the Good News of God's boundless love and radical inclusion, undeterred by fear or oppression.

Let us draw strength from our shared faith and the promise of God's abiding presence. As we navigate these challenges together, may we remain steadfast in hope and united in love, ever confident that *"perfect love casts out fear"* (1 John 4:18).

With deepest love and unwavering support,

Most Rev. George R. Lucey, FCM
Presiding Bishop

October 18, 2024
Feast of Saint Luke, Evangelist

> *For in the one Spirit we were all baptized into one body—Jews or Greeks, slaves or free—and we were all made to drink of one Spirit. Indeed, the body does not consist of one member but of many."*
>
> *"Now you are the body of Christ and individually members of it."*
>
> *- 1 Corinthians 12:13*

Dear Sisters and Brothers in Christ,

In the name of the Father, and of the Son, + and of the Holy Spirit.

May the peace of our Lord Jesus Christ be with you always.

I write to you today as we prepare to exercise one of our most significant privileges and responsibilities as citizens of the United States of America. As Catholics, our consciences are shaped and informed by the person of Jesus Christ. Our relationship with Him is rooted in our experience of His compassion, forgiveness, and mercy. We follow a Savior who has a preferential option for the poor and marginalized. In a time of growing political division, it is often the poor and vulnerable who suffer the most—whether through economic injustice, lack of access to basic services, or through scapegoating and demonization. As followers of Christ, we are called to prioritize their needs and to recognize the face of Christ in them (Matthew 25:40).

As a Christian community, our baptismal covenant reminds us that we are called to be prophets in our own time. Our faith serves as a guide in navigating these challenging times in our country. By grounding our political understanding in the tenets of our faith, as outlined in Scripture and Catholic Social Teaching, we can make informed decisions about our social responsibilities to one another.

Our response to the increasing levels of division, conflict, and even violence in society must be as peacemakers. This means engaging in respectful dialogue, especially with those we disagree with, and remembering that God loves them as much as He loves us. In the Sermon on the Mount, Jesus blesses those who work for peace, calling them "children of God" (Matthew 5:9). Peace is not merely the absence of conflict but the presence of justice, mercy, and love. As the Body of Christ, we are called to act peacefully and invite others, by our example, to safely engage in the political process.

To be peacemakers today, we must examine our own attitudes and actions, ensuring they align with the peace of the Kingdom. St. Francis of Assisi, reflecting on Psalm 147, reminds us that we are "called to heal wounds, to unite what has fallen apart, and to bring home those who have lost their way." As members of the

American National Catholic Church, we must rise to this challenge, embodying these teachings, fostering unity, and working for the common good.

In this time of political unrest and threats of violence, our Church is called not only to proclaim the virtues of justice and mercy but also to act on them. Every moment invites us to respond with mercy, justice, and tender love. Let us unite our prayers with all people of good faith, asking the Holy Spirit to inspire us to be witnesses to Gospel values and to empower us to act with the courage of our faith.

As members of the American National Catholic Church, we have a unique opportunity to be a beacon of hope, love, and unity in a fractured world. In this moment of heightened division, the teachings of our faith offer us a clear path forward. Let us reject hatred, build bridges, and work tirelessly for justice and peace.

May God bless you and strengthen you for this holy work.

In Christ,

Most Rev. George R. Lucey, FCM
Presiding Bishop

August 28, 2024

Memorial of Saint Augustine, Bishop and Doctor of the Church

> *"Long ago I gave these commands to my people: 'You must see that justice is done and must show kindness and mercy to one another. Do not oppress widows, orphans, foreigners who live among you, or anyone else in need."*
> *- Zechariah 7:9*

Called to Be Witnesses of Christ in a Time of Division

Dear Brothers and Sisters in Christ,

In the name of the Father and of the Son + and of the Holy Spirit

As we approach another season of political campaigning, we find ourselves amidst a cacophony of voices, each striving to capture our attention and loyalty. The airwaves, social media, and public discourse are filled with messages that often appeal to our fears, prejudices, and divisions. In this charged atmosphere, it is easy to forget the higher calling to which we, as followers of Christ, are committed.

The social teaching of the Catholic Church offers us a timeless guide, rooted in the Gospel, for how we might navigate these turbulent times with grace, wisdom, and faith. It reminds us that our engagement in the public square must be shaped by our Christian values and by our unwavering commitment to justice, peace, and the dignity of every human being.

1. *The Dignity of the Human Person*

   At the heart of Catholic social teaching is the belief in the inherent dignity of every human person. This conviction must inform all our actions, including how we engage in political discourse. We are called to resist the temptation to dehumanize those with whom we disagree and instead to seek out the image of God in each person we encounter. In our words and actions, let us be witnesses to a love that transcends political divisions, recognizing that our true citizenship is in heaven (Philippians 3:20).

2. *The Common Good*

   The pursuit of the common good is a fundamental principle that should guide our political engagement. We are called to look beyond narrow self-interest and to consider the wellbeing of all, especially the most vulnerable among us. In a time when political rhetoric often divides us into opposing camps, we must resist the urge to retreat into echo chambers that reinforce our biases. Instead, let us seek dialogue and collaboration, working together to build a society that reflects the values of justice, compassion, and mutual respect

3. *Solidarity*

Our faith calls us to a deep sense of solidarity with all people, recognizing that we are all members of one human family. This solidarity must extend to those who are marginalized, oppressed, or forgotten by society. As we engage in the political process, let us remember that our actions should be motivated not by partisan loyalty, but by a desire to lift up those who are most in need. In doing so, we fulfill Christ's command to love our neighbor as ourselves (Mark 12:31).

4. *Option for the Poor*

The preferential option for the poor is a call to prioritize the needs of the most vulnerable in our society. As Christians, we are challenged to advocate for policies that promote social justice, economic fairness, and the protection of human rights. In our political decisions, let us be guided by a concern for those who are most often ignored or exploited by systems of power.

5. *Peace and Reconciliation*

Finally, we are called to be peacemakers in a world that often glorifies conflict and division. Our Lord Jesus Christ taught us that blessed are the peacemakers, for they shall be called children of God (Matthew 5:9). As we navigate this election season, let us be voices of reason and reconciliation, striving to build bridges rather than walls, and seeking to heal the wounds of division in our communities and our nation.

Dear friends, as we engage in the political process, let us do so with a spirit of prayer and discernment, asking the Holy Spirit to guide our hearts and minds. Let us remember that our ultimate allegiance is to Christ, and that our political engagement must always reflect the values of the Gospel.

May the Lord bless you and keep you in His peace during this time and may we all be strengthened in our commitment to live out our faith in the public square.

Yours in Christ,

Most Rev. George R. Lucey, FCM
Presiding Bishop

June 6, 2024

Presiding Bishop's Statement in Support of Peace Talks in the Middle East
How good and pleasant it is when brothers and sisters live together in unity! It
is like precious oil poured on the head, running down on the beard, running
down on Aaron's beard, down upon the collar of his robes.

- Psalm 133: 1-2

Dear Brother and Sisters,

Peace!

I begin many of my letters and formal communications with the salutation of
"Peace." I use it as an invitation for us to be free of anxiety and as a reminder to
myself that as I write or speak, I do so with the hope that my words invite peace
and not discord.

The word "peace" in Hebrew is pregnant with meaning. It is a statement about
being "at peace" with oneself, a desire on the part of the person offering it for the
other to be whole, to be complete, to be well, and—most fundamentally—it is a
belief in our need for reconciliation with God.

Social psychology informs us that violence toward another person or group begins
with "anti-locution," demeaning the "other" to make them less than human.

Jesus, three times in the Gospel of John, in his post-resurrection appearances to the
disciples, counters this phenomenon by asking us, his followers, to face our fears
of one another and unlock the doors of our minds and hearts to those whom we
most fear (John 20:19).

The second time Jesus appears, he offers us peace as a source of strength,
reminding us that God is close to the broken-hearted, and as a lingering sense of
his presence with us until the end (John 20:26). The final appearance recorded in
the Upper Room provides the foundation of inclusion, as a statement of the unity
of purpose and mission which we are all called to pursue (John 20:21).

As Christians, we know that to be children of God calls us to be peacemakers. We
in the American National Catholic Church join in prayer and action for all those
working for peace in the Middle East. We celebrate and are in solidarity with all
who are willing to walk in peace with each other.

Memorial of the Presentation of Mary

November 21, 2022

A Pastoral Response to the shooting at Club Q

As the Christian community prepares to celebrate the liturgical season of Advent, a time to reflect on the themes of joy, hope, peace, and love, we prepare our hearts and minds for the celebration of Christmas; the mystery of the Incarnation; we as a nation are challenged by yet another act of gun violence and slaughter.

As we witness another incidence of hatred toward one of our LGBTQI communities and, elsewhere our Jewish brothers and sisters, we might be tempted to cry out with the prophet Habakkuk, *"How long, Lord, must I call for help, but you do not listen? Or cry out to you, "Violence!" but you do not save?" (Hab 1.2).* We might despair at the seemingly never ending toxic mix of hate coupled with guns and acknowledge that these attacks stand in stark contrast to the Advent invitation to hold on to God's promise that, *"Justice shall flourish in his time, and fullness of peace forever." (Psalm 72.7)*

The American National Catholic Church is committed to being a witness to the all-inclusive and extravagant love of God made flesh in the person of Jesus Christ. This Advent, in the midst of this tragedy, we can be courageous in our acts of inclusion and commit ourselves to be steadfast followers of the Prince of Peace.

25 May 2022

Memorial of St. Bede the Venerable

In the name of the Father, + the Son, and the Holy Spirit!

When Matthew the evangelist tried to describe King Herod's slaughter of the Bethlehem innocents, the recollection of the event left him so dumbstruck with horror that he could only quote a passage from the prophet Jeremiah:

Thus saith the Lord: A voice was heard in Ramah, lamentation and bitter weeping; Rachel, weeping for her children, refused to be comforted for her children, because they were no more.

Once again, there's weeping in the land, this time over the savage murder of school children in Uvalde, Texas. The tragedy is second only to Sandy Hook in the sheer number of victims. It's the 27th school shooting this year alone, and it comes just days after the tragic murder of 10 people in a Buffalo store.

The heartbreaking regularity of gun deaths in this nation, and especially the murder of innocent children, breaks our hearts and wearies our spirit. We cry out with the psalmist:

How long, O Lord, will you forget us forever?

How long will you hide your face from us?

At this point we know little about the Uvalde shooter, but it's hard not to imagine that he was psychologically ill. Yet we know that the percentage of mental illness in the United States is comparable to percentages in other countries. What isn't comparable is the easy accessibility of weapons in this nation. There are 393 million firearms in civilian hands in the United States, a number that outstrips the total population by nearly 70 million.

We are drowning in a sea of guns, which makes tragedies like Uvalde all the more likely. And Rachel still weeps.

As followers of the Prince of Peace, we must reaffirm and strengthen our alliances with all people of good will to persuade lawmakers to finally, at long last, better regulate both the types of weapons on the market and their accessibility. We must do everything we can to reach out to troubled individuals, especially youths, who might be tempted to duplicate the carnage of Columbine, Sandy Hook, and Uvalde. We simply must take as our own the task of ridding the nation of the blight of gun deaths. We are indeed the keepers of our sisters and our brothers, especially those who, like our children, are most at risk.

So let us pray for these latest victims and their families. Let us pray also for the young man responsible for this tragedy. But let's roll up our sleeves and put our faith in action by at long last stopping the carnage.

Then Rachel's weeping will finally cease.

12 January 2021

Feast of Aelred of Rievaulx

The Most Reverend George R. Lucey, FCM,

Presiding Bishop of the American National Catholic Church,

Calls on Mr. Trump to Resign

In the name of the Father, and of the +Son, and of the Holy Spirit!

Dear Sisters and Brothers in Christ:

The insurrection that resulted in the storming of the Capitol and the death of at least five persons, instigated by the incendiary and false insistence on the part of Mr. Trump and his allies that the November election was invalid, is not simply a body blow to American democracy. It's also a mockery of cherished Christian values.

The physical and verbal violence that crescendoed on January 6 is antithetical to the fundamental principles of Catholic social teaching: respect for human dignity and human rights, the complementarity of personal and social responsibilities in pursuit of the common good, and a solidarity with all persons expressed in love, compassion, service, and justice.

Mr. Trump's inflammatory and hateful rhetoric, which launched his campaign and continued right up to last week's debacle; his apparent aversion to truth-telling; his vilification of anyone who disagrees with or displeases him; his willingness to abuse presidential prerogative by engaging in strong arm tactics; his prioritizing his personal interests over the nation's; and, finally, his direct responsibility for the shameful insurrection, demonstrate his unfitness to be president.

Accordingly, I call upon Mr. Trump to immediately resign for the good of the nation he has so damaged.

I also invite my fellow Christians, regardless of denomination, to pray that the threat of domestic violence over the next few days dissipates, that people of good will join together to nonviolently resist those who would subvert democracy, and that all of us allow ourselves to be guided by the better angels of our nature rather than anger and fear.

Today is the feast of the twelfth-century saint Aelred of Rievaulx, author of a treatise in which he argued that friendship is a sacrament of God's love. Friendship, he believed, creates a bond of dialogue, reciprocity, and self-giving that reflects the love between Father, Son, and Holy Spirit. My prayer is that our nation can begin to unite in the friendship that Aelred saw as essential to individual well-being, social stability, and communion with the Creator.

The Most Reverend George R. Lucey, FCM
Presiding Bishop

28 October 2020

Feast of Saints Simon & Jude

Resisting the Normalization of Indifference

A Pastoral Letter from the Most Reverend George R. Lucey, FCM,

Presiding Bishop

In the name of the Father, Son +, and Holy Spirit!

Dear sisters and brothers in Christ:

The recent revelation that the U.S. government is unable to locate the mothers and fathers of some 545 migrant children taken from their asylum-seeking parents at the Mexican border should weigh heavily on the hearts of each American.

Yet barely a week after the story broke, the news cycle has moved on and we go about our daily lives as if these innocent children, who may never see their parents again, aren't suffering.

This sorrowful state of affairs reflects a broader cultural and spiritual malaise: the normalization of indifference. Although the Internet makes us more aware than ever before of the suffering of people around the world and in our own vicinities, we seem increasingly jaded and unresponsive to the news. After shedding a few quick and sentimental tears over the misfortunes of others we quickly resume our normal business. It is what the Protestant theologian and martyr Dietrich Bonheoffer, who coined the expression "cheap grace," might've called "cheap compassion." It costs us nothing.

The indifference to suffering which is in danger of becoming endemic in our culture isn't garden-variety apathy, laziness, or inaction. It's a pernicious denial of the God-given dignity of all persons. When we remain unmoved by the misfortunes of others, we signal that we don't really see them as fellow human beings worthy of genuine compassion and love. Their suffering simply isn't worth getting worked up about, even if they happen to be 545 children victimized by institutionalized xenophobia and orphaned by bureaucratic incompetence.

But my sisters and brothers, we Christians know that our normalization of indifference is in fact spiritually and morally abnormal. The prophets of ancient Judah and Israel, our Lord in his life and teachings, the apostles and the saints, and the great councils of the Church, all remind us that we indeed are siblings to one another, that the suffering of any diminishes us all, and that as members of God's family we are called to look out for one another, not so much out of a sense of duty as from the call of love.

This is especially the case when it comes to people who come to us as refugees seeking relief from violence and poverty. As Paul VI reminded us in his Populorum Progressio: On the Development of Peoples, it is "at once a duty of human solidarity and Christian charity" to treat anyone seeking asylum with "genuine and effective Christian charity and the highest spiritual values." We have not honored this duty when it comes to the border children who have lost their parents. We have failed them, and in doing so have failed the God who loves them.

My prayer is that the good and gracious Lord who now suffers alongside those 545 frightened and grieving children will break open our hearts of flinty indifference and grant us the gift of genuinely feeling their pain and the pain of the entire world. May the God of all who suffer, of all who are lost and forlorn, and of all who feel abandoned, fill us with such compassion, willingness to sacrifice, nobility of character, and kindness that these virtues, rather than indifference, become the norms which define our culture.

The Most Reverend George R. Lucey, FCM
Presiding Bishop

Presiding Bishop George Lucey on the Murder of George Floyd

30 May 2020

Solemnity of Pentecost

In the name + of the Father, Son, and Holy Spirit!

"I can't breathe." So gasped George Floyd shortly before he was murdered by a Minneapolis police officer last Monday. "I can't breathe."

This isn't the first time an African American man has uttered these terrible words. Six years ago, Eric Garner said the same thing as he was throttled to death by New York City police on Staten Island.

Today the Church celebrates Pentecost, the descent of the Holy Spirit. I've always been struck by the fact that in both Hebrew and Greek, the languages of the Bible, the word for spirit also can be translated as "breath" and "wind." God's spirit or wind breathes order upon the chaotic void. (Gen 1:2) God breathes life into the primordial couple. (Gen 2:7) The prophet Ezekiel tells us that God's breath or spirit reanimates dry bones. (Ezekiel 37:5) And at Pentecost, the Risen Lord breathes the Holy Spirit into humanity. (John 20:22)

Breath is life, spirit, vitality, the living presence of God. To rob another person of it is a horrible offense against both the God who lovingly breathes us into existence and the mortals whose God-given breath our hatred stifles.

Racial violence, inflicted on George Floyd, Eric Garner, Sandra Blands, Breonna Taylor, and countless other African American men, women, and children, is just such an offense.

As Christians, you and I are called to honor the Spirit of God and the vitality of life in our sisters and brothers without exception. We cannot do that if we turn a blind eye to the institutional racism that infects our culture, much less the racial prejudice which we ourselves may be harboring, perhaps without even being consciously aware of doing so. We cannot do that unless we confess our guilt, repent of it, and work to make sure that public policies and our own behavior change so that equal protection of the law is truly practiced and enforced no matter the color of skin. Only in this way can we live in a society where all people can live without fear of the breath of life being throttled from them, whether physically, economically or through other structures, institutions and agencies of our society.

My sisters and brothers and people of good will everywhere: I ask you to join me in prayerful contrition for our complicity in the racial violence, which burdens this nation. I ask you to prayerfully, stalwartly, compassionately, and nonviolently witness for justice and stand against the bigotry institutionalized in too many of our legal, economic, and social structures.

In doing so, we honor God's spirit, breath, life. In doing so, we truly celebrate Pentecost.

The Most Reverend George R. Lucey, FCM
Presiding Bishop

ANCC Presiding Bishop's Plea for Peace between the United States and Iran

8 January 2020

Wednesday after Epiphany

In the name + of the Father, Son, and Holy Spirit!

It's sorrowful that in this season of Christmas, a time in which Christians around the world joyfully celebrate the Nativity of the Prince of Peace, simmering hostilities between the United States and Iran erupted in violence: the White House-sanctioned assassination of an Iranian general and Iran's retaliatory missile strike against two U.S. air bases.

For now, at least, the immediate threat of armed escalation has been put on hold. But the United States and Iran—and, for that matter, the entire world—were taken to the brink of all-out war by this latest clash. Regrettably, given the unabatedly hostile relationship between Washington and Teheran, war remains a real possibility.

St. John XXIII's 1963 encyclical Pacem in Terris (Peace on Earth) was written just months after the Cuban Missile Crisis brought the world to the very edge of war. In it, St. John urged the world's political leaders to abandon strongarm tactics and saber-rattling for the gentler and ultimately more fruitful tasks of diplomacy and international cooperation. He wrote:

> *May God enlighten the rulers of peoples so that in addition to their solicitude for the proper welfare of their citizens, they may guarantee and defend the great gift of peace; may He enkindle the wills of all, so that they may overcome the barriers that divide, cherish the bonds of mutual charity, understand others, and pardon those who have done them wrong; by virtue of his action, may all peoples of the earth become as brothers, and may the most longed-for peace blossom forth and reign always among them.*

It is my fervent prayer that Mr. Trump and the leaders of Iran, as well as the peoples of both our nations, "overcome the barriers that divide" by sincerely seeking a peaceful means of resolving differences. I join with all persons of good will in urging representatives from both sides to meet immediately to end the half-century of hostility that has led us to the frightening brink upon which we now stand.

May we honor the Prince of Peace by building harmony between our nations.

The Most Reverend George R. Lucey, FCM

Presiding Bishop

A Pastoral Letter from Presiding Bishop George Lucey, FCM, on the Mass Shootings in California, Texas, and Ohio

August 5, 2019

Feast of the Dedication of St. Mary Major

In the name + of the Father, Son, and Holy Spirit!

Once more, the nation reels in stunned dismay at gun violence, on horrific display no fewer than three times in the space of a single week. Innocent men, women, and children in Gilroy CA, El Paso TX, and Dayton OH are the latest victims of the rage and hatred that roams the land like a ravenous lion seeking prey. (1 Peter 5:1)

The people of the American National Catholic Church offer heartfelt prayers for those killed and wounded in these three tragedies. We offer prayers as well for their loved ones, for officers of the law who stopped the attacks and EMT and emergency room personnel who treated victims, and for all past survivors of similar tragedies forced to relive their trauma again and again whenever a new shooting occurs.

Prayer is more than appropriate because we are people of faith. As Christians who worship a Messiah of peace, compassion, and love, and who was himself cruelly murdered by agents of violence, we turn to the Lord in all circumstances, but especially in troubled ones like this.

But as Christ's disciples, we know that we're called to complement our prayers with action. The Lord tells us that whenever we come to the aid of those in need, we serve him as well. (Matthew 25: 34-40) As St. Teresa of Avila reminds us, we are the hands and feet of God.

Between them, the three killers exemplify two toxins eating away at this nation's moral fiber: the easy availability and out-of-control abundance of semi-and fully automatic weapons, and the rise of white nationalism. As of now, the motives of the Gilroy and Dayton shooters remain mysterious. But we do know that the weapons they used were designed for rapid kills. In the case of the El Paso tragedy, the shooter's motives are clearly stated in a white nationalist statement he posted online shortly before his rampage. It indicated rage at what he styled the "Hispanic invasion" of Texas.

I call upon Christians everywhere—and indeed all persons, regardless of their faith—to insist that local, state, and federal government leaders act swiftly and decisively to enact restrictions on the private ownership of semi- and fully automatic weapons.

I call upon the president to cease his recklessly incendiary language about immigrants and repent the anger and ethnic violence that his public statements have encouraged during his time in office.

And I humbly and with grieving heart ask Mary and all the saints to intercede on behalf of this hurting, bleeding nation, that everyone who dwells in it or who come to its borders in search of asylum might live without fear of violence and be treated as the beloved children of God which they are.

The Most Reverend George R. Lucey, FCM
Presiding Bishop

28 October 2018

In the name + of the Father, Son, and Holy Spirit!

Once again it is my sad duty as Presiding Bishop of the American National Catholic Church to express my shock and sorrow at another senseless mass shooting. On Saturday, October 27, a gunman entered the Tree of Life or L'Simcha synagogue in Pittsburgh and opened fire on the congregants gathered there for worship, killing eleven sons and daughters of the Covenant and wounding many more. May Father Abraham hug them to his bosom and stand with them before ha-Shem.

I am immensely saddened by this violence perpetrated upon our Jewish sisters and brothers as they celebrated Shabbat. The violent loss of life is always an unspeakable tragedy, but even more so when it occurs in houses dedicated to God.

I am also bitterly disappointed by the current administration's failure to encourage, through exhortation, executive order, and policy, an end to the violence shattering this nation.

As Christians, we are people of hope. We have faith in the vision of the prophets and the promise of Jesus Christ that one day all tears will be wiped away, all brokenness will be repaired, and all who are lost will return home. God willing, our faith will embolden us to step into the breach created by the administration's refusal to encourage civility, dialogue, and empathy, and to speak and act in peaceful and loving ways.

Please join me in praying that the anger infecting this nation will soon lessen. And please join me and people of good will everywhere in saying kaddish for our sisters and brothers who yesterday became hate's latest victims as they worshipped the God of mercy and love.

The Most Reverend George R. Lucey, FCM
Presiding George

28 May 2018

A Pastoral Letter from Presiding Bishop George Lucey, FCM,

on the Crisis of Immigrant Children

"Am I my brother's keeper?" (Gen 4:9)

We read in the Hebrew scriptures that this is the question Cain, murderer of his brother Abel, threw at God in an attempt to justify his bloodguilt. It has been on my mind these last few weeks as we learn about the harm our nation's increasingly harsh immigration policies are inflicting on innocent children.

Last month, Department of Health and Human Services official Steven Wagner testified that his agency has lost track of nearly 1,500 children who crossed the U.S.-Mexico border unaccompanied by adults and were subsequently placed with sponsors. Only 85 of the missing children have been accounted for thus far.

The tragedy of this situation is compounded by remarks recently made by Attorney General Jeff Sessions. Speaking in Arizona and California, Mr. Sessions insisted that our nation "cannot take everyone on this planet who is in a difficult situation." Consequently, he continued, "If you cross the border unlawfully … then we will prosecute you. If you smuggle an illegal alien across the border, then we'll prosecute you. … If you're smuggling a child, then we're going to prosecute you, and that child will be separated from you, probably, as required by law."

His conclusion? "If you don't want your child separated, then don't bring them (sic) across the border illegally. It's not our fault that somebody does that."

In other words, we're not the keepers of your children.

Just as Abel's spilt blood cried out to heaven, so the suffering that our immigration policies inflict upon children will testify against us as a nation. All of us—people of faith and people of good will who may have no faith—are duty-bound to welcome and protect sojourners who come to our doors in need of hospitality. Surely that duty can't be any more obvious than when the well-being of children is at stake. With due respect to Mr. Sessions, if we turn them away, or fail to protect them once they're in the country, it is our fault.

An essential principle of Christian morality is communality: the belief that we are siblings to one another by virtue of our shared divine parentage, and that consequently no one is outside the family circle of moral concern, especially those who, like children, are most vulnerable. I pray with all my heart that we and our elected officials will be moved to take this principle seriously and come to see that all of us are indeed one another's keeper.

Most Rev. George R. Lucey, FCM
Presiding Bishop
The American National Catholic Church

15 January 2018

A Pastoral Letter from Presiding Bishop George R. Lucey, FCM,

on the Sin of Racism

Racism is a terrible sin, founded on the pernicious falsehood that some human beings are inferior simply because of the color of their skin and hence are undeserving of respectful and fair treatment. It is both dismaying and disheartening that such an obvious statement should have to be made in the year 2018. But reported comments by Donald Trump, some uttered in June 2017 and others just this week, clearly indicate that even the leader of the United States is susceptible to the spiritual poison of racism.

The president's remarks are especially troubling because they implicitly bestow a stamp of approval upon racist sentiments, expressions, and behavior. This encourages—or at least fails to discourage—similar responses from his constituents. This is far from good leadership.

There can be no doubt that racism is contrary to Judeo-Christian values. The book of Genesis tells us (1:26) that God created humans in his own image, thereby bestowing on each and every member of the human family intrinsic dignity and value. Our Lord underscores this point when he tells us that, "as you did it to one of the least of these my brothers and sisters, you did it to me." (Mt 25:40)

In Gaudium et spes (27.1), the Vatican-II Council affirmed the Lord's teaching that all persons are equal in the eyes of God and should be treated with fairness and respect. "This council lays stress on reverence for humans; everyone must consider their every neighbor without exception as another self, taking into account first of all their lives and the means necessary to living them with dignity."

In his essay "The Weight of Glory," the 20th-century Anglican author C.S. Lewis made a similar point when he wrote that none of us has ever met an "ordinary" person; each individual, by virtue of his or her likeness to God, is "extraordinary" and deserving of our respect.

It is my fervent prayer that all Christians and, indeed, peoples of all or no faith examine their consciences to discern whether and to what extent they harbor racist sentiments. Let us pray for one another, and especially for Donald Trump, with God's help, we may learn to judge others by the content of their characters and not the color of their skins. This was the dream of Dr. Martin Luther King, Jr. It is mine as well, and I believe it is also the Lord's.

Signed on Martin Luther King, Jr. Day

Most Rev. George R. Lucey, FCM
Presiding Bishop
The American National Catholic Church

14 August 2017

Memorial of Saint Maximilian Kolbe

A Pastoral Letter from Presiding Bishop George R. Lucey, FCM,
on Warlike Rhetoric and White Nationalism

+ In the name of the Father, and of the Son, and of the Holy Spirit!

The past week has been one that surely has grieved and frightened all persons of good will.

First, the current president alarmed the world with breathtakingly bellicose threats directed at the North Korean regime. In what were reportedly extemporaneous remarks, Mr. Trump warned that the U.S. was prepared to inflict on North Korea "fire, fury, and frankly power the likes of which this world has never seen before." The president's remarks, in response to news that North Korea is now able to launch a nuclear-tipped ICBM missile, led to a speedy and heated escalation of threats and warlike rhetoric from both sides.

Analysts worry that Mr. Trump's intemperate words have brought the U.S. closer to a nuclear confrontation than it's been since the 1963 Cuban Missile Crisis.

In his encyclical Pacem in Terris, released at the height of the Cold War and addressed to Christians and non-Christians alike, St. John XXIII urged the world's leaders to seek the common good by exercising genuine moral authority instead of "govern[ing] solely or mainly by means of threats and intimidation" (#48). As a Vatican diplomat for much of his adult life, St. John was well acquainted with the dangerous consequences of warlike rhetoric in fraught times of international tension.

The unthinkable horror of nuclear confrontation only underscores the wisdom of his position.

It is my fervent hope and prayer that God enlightens the minds and opens the hearts of the U.S. and North Korea leaders to lead them away from their perilous course of mutual threats and intimidation before they reach a point of no-return.

Second, the nation witnessed a truly abominable display of hatred and violence in Charlottesville, VA, this weekend, when Klansmen, Nazis, and white nationalists marched through the streets to proclaim their own toxic mix of threats and intimidation. Tragically but predictably, their hatred and rage spawned violence that led to the murder of a young woman and the wounding of a score of others.

Thankfully, the vast majority of citizens and politicians in the nation are shocked by this brutal display of hatred. Christians, it is to be hoped, are even more so. We worship and proclaim a God whose incarnation was heralded by angels with greetings of peace and good will to all, and whose resurrected message was likewise one of peace. As his disciples, we are called—we are obliged—to be advocates of peace, exemplifying it not only in our personal behavior but also opposing firmly, but not hatefully or forcibly, those who would threaten it with bellicose intimidation or rupture it with overt violence. For all those who follow the path of violence eventually arrive at death and destruction. As the psalmist tells us,

> *They dig a pitfall, dig it deep;*
>
> *and in the trap they have made they will fall.*
>
> *Their malice will recoil on themselves;*
>
> *on their own heads their violence will fall.*
>
> *(7: 15-16)*

As followers of the Prince of Peace, let us join with all persons of good will to recommit ourselves to peace and life, and reaffirm our opposition to violence and death.

Signed on this Memorial of St. Maximilian Kolbe, the Franciscan martyr who witnessed to Christ's peace by sacrificing himself for others at Auschwitz.

Most Rev. George R. Lucey, FCM
Presiding Bishop
The American National Catholic Church

5 June 2017

A Pastoral Letter From Ancc Presiding Bishop George R. Lucey, Fcm, On The President'S Withdraw From The Paris Accord

+ In the name of the Father, and of the Son, and of the Holy Spirit!

The psalmist tells us that "the earth is the Lord's, and all that dwells therein." This reminds us of the fact, proclaimed in Genesis and affirmed by centuries of Hebraic and Christian tradition, that God's creation is good and that we humans are called to be grateful stewards of it.

Unhappily, the good earth is in trouble. The vast majority of climate scientists conclude that human activity, particularly the extensive use of fossil fuels, is accelerating global warming's extreme weather patterns, rising sea levels, and glacial erosion to an alarming degree. The danger to the planet also poses a grave threat to human well-being.

It is, therefore, profoundly regrettable that the President has chosen to withdraw the United States from the Paris Accord, the unprecedented agreement that pledges the nations of the world to curtail greenhouse gas emissions. Only two nations, Syria and Nicaragua, refused to sign the Accord.

The U.S. now joins them.

The withdrawal from the Paris Accord is accompanied by the President's refusal to honor the U.S. pledge to the Green Climate Fund. The Fund offers financial aid to developing nations, which will be unduly penalized by a reduction of fossil fuel use.

The President's decisions not only display a disregard for the health of the planet, but also suggest an unwillingness to accept responsibility for the fact that the U.S. has the largest carbon footprint in history and remains today the globe's second largest emitter of carbon dioxide.

The American National Catholic Church joins all people of good will throughout the world in the fervent hope that the current President will awaken to the obligation, born of love for the Creator and creation, to cherish and protect the environment.

Most Rev. George R. Lucey, FCM

Presiding Bishop

The American National Catholic Church

29 October 2015

Feast of St. Narcissus of Jerusalem

ANCC Bishop Calls for an End to Gun Violence

+ The grace of our Lord Jesus Christ, the love of God, and the fellowship of the Holy Spirit be with you all.

On behalf of the People of God and the clergy of the American National Catholic Church(ANCC), I wish to express grave moral and spiritual concern over what has been correctly called an "epidemic" of gun violence in the United States.

In two days, Catholic and Protestant Christians will celebrate the Solemnity of All Saints, in which we remember and honor those who have gone to be with the Lord. It is appropriate that we call to mind all the thousands who have died from gun violence.

Between 1 January 2013 and 2 October 2015—a total of 1,004 days—1,260 people have been killed and another 3,606 have been wounded by guns. In that same period of time, there have been 994 mass shootings.[1] The total of all deaths in U.S. wars, from Lexington to Afghanistan, is nearly 1,400,000. (The latest casualty fell in the final week of October.) Staggering as that number is, it's in fact slightly less than approximately more than 1,500,000 people killed by guns since 1968.[2]

Gun violence has become so commonplace that one British journalist concluded three years ago that the U.S. is in a de facto civil war.[3] After the latest mass killing on 2nd of October, this time at Oregon's Umpqua Community College, a stunned President Obama spoke for many in this nation when he lamented that "somehow this has become routine…We've become numb to this… It cannot be this easy for someone who wants to inflict harm on someone else to get his or her hands on a gun."[4]

---

[1] " 994 mass shootings in 1,004 days: this is what America's gun crisis looks like," The Guardian (2 October 2015).

[2] "American War and Military Operations Casualties: Lists and Statistics," Congressional Research Service (2 January 2015): http://www.fas.org/sgp/crs/natsec/RL32492.pdf; Louis Jacobson, "More Americans killed by guns since 1968 than in all U.S. wars, columnist Nicholas Kristof writes," Punditfact (27 August 2015): http://www.politifact.com/punditfact/statements/2015/aug/27/nicholas-kristof/more-americans-killed-guns-1968-all-wars-says-colu/

[3] Henry Potter, "American gun use is out of control. Shouldn't the world intervene?", The Guardian (21 September 2013).

[4] Maya Rhodan, "Obama Says Mass Shootings Have Become 'Routine 'in America", Time (1 October 2015).

This tragic state of affairs shocks and grieves every person of good will. As followers of the Prince of Peace, we Christians are especially saddened that so many acts of gun violence darken each and every day of the calendar.

In 1963, Saint John XXIII, whom God inspired to convene the Second Vatican Council, released Pacem in Terris, one of the most important encyclicals of the twentieth century. Written at the height of the Cold War and shortly after the Cuban Missile Crisis, John's encyclical was an eloquent plea for an end to the out-of-control nuclear arms race between the United States and the Soviet Union. The Cold War has ended. But Saint John's call for8disarmament fifty years ago also speaks to the epidemic of gun violence plaguing this nation today.

John XXIII pointed out that genuine peace between nations can't be founded on the distrust that prompts the stockpiling of weapons. Instead, peace must be grounded in mutual trust. Such a state of affairs, he wrote, "not only is dictated by common sense, but is in itself most desirable and most fruitful of good," as well as being in accord with the regulatory principles of "truth, justice, and vigorous and sincere co-operation."

The extraordinary proliferation of firearms in the U.S.—currently more than 300 million— is a stockpiling and as threatening to personal safety today as nuclear stockpiling was to international safety a generation ago. In both cases, the sheer quantity of weapons seduces us with a false sense of security that blinds us to the very real possibility of their frequent abuse. We put ourselves at physical risk if we do nothing to curtail gun violence. We damage our spiritual wellbeing too.

I invite my fellow Christians in all denominations and jurisdictions to join me in praying for legislation that aims at doing something about the proliferation of guns and gun violence in our nation. As Saint John XXIII said, Christians are called to "co-operate in the effort to banish fear." In this nation, right now, we honor that obligation to God and to our fellow citizens by controlling the number as well as the kinds of guns available. Our shared hope, in the beautiful words of the prophet Isaiah (60:18), is that "Violence shall no more be heard in your land, devastation or destruction within your borders; you shall call your walls Salvation, and your gates Praise."

Yours in Christ,

+ George R. Lucey, FCM

Most Rev. George R. Lucey, FCM
Presiding Bishop
The American National Catholic Church

Discussion Questions

1. How do these pastoral letters embody Vatican II's call to read the "signs of the times" without collapsing theology into politics?

2. In what ways do the letters distinguish between partisan advocacy and moral witness grounded in Catholic Social Teaching?

3. How does the ANCC's treatment of violence, racism, and migration reflect a sacramental understanding of human dignity?

4. Where do you see continuity—and development—with earlier Catholic social encyclicals such as *Populorum Progressio* or *Fratelli Tutti*?

5. What challenges arise when the Church speaks prophetically in moments of public crisis, and how do these letters navigate those tensions?

Chapter II:
The People of God and Ministry
(Lumen Gentium)

Introduction to the Letters in This Category

The letters in this section are unified by an ecclesiological vision rooted in *Lumen Gentium*'s recovery of the Church as the People of God. They attend to the Church's inner life—its ministries, leadership, failures, hopes, and ongoing conversion—always with the conviction that the Church exists not for itself but for the sake of the Gospel.

Vatican II decisively shifted Catholic self-understanding away from an exclusively hierarchical model toward one of communion, co-responsibility, and shared baptismal dignity. These pastoral letters reflect that shift by addressing clergy and laity alike as partners in mission, each called to holiness and service in accordance with their gifts. Whether expressing gratitude, calling for repentance, or offering guidance in moments of transition, the letters here assume that authority in the Church is fundamentally pastoral rather than juridical.

Particularly significant within this category are letters that confront institutional sin, especially in relation to clerical abuse and failures of accountability. Their inclusion underscores a core conciliar insight: that the Church is holy, yet always in need of purification. Fidelity to Christ demands truth-telling, humility, and reform, not defensiveness or denial.

Read together, these letters invite the faithful to see the Church as a pilgrim people—wounded yet graced—continually being shaped by the Spirit into a more authentic sign of God's reign. They articulate an ANCC ecclesiology that is recognizably Catholic, deeply conciliar, and resolutely committed to communion over clericalism.

March 22 2025

A Pastoral Letter to the People of God and the Clergy of the American National Catholic Church

Lent 2025

> *"Wash yourselves, make yourselves clean.*
> *Take your wrongdoing out of my sight.*
> *Cease to do evil. Learn to do good, search for justice,*
> *help the oppressed, be just to the orphan, plead for the widow.*
> *Come now, let us talk this over, says the Lord.*
> *Though your sins are like scarlet, they shall be as white as snow;*
> *though they are red as crimson, they shall be like wool."*

—Isaiah 1:16–18

Dear Sisters and Brothers in Christ,

In the Name of the Father, and of the +Son, and of the Holy Spirit. At the end of this Second Week of Lent, I wanted to write to you my sincerest hopes for a grace-filled Lenten journey as we travel with Jesus to Jerusalem, to His Passion and death and to rejoice with Him at the Resurrection.

As we enter this holy season of Lent, the Church invites us into a time of *metanoia*—a profound change of heart, mind, and life. In this sacred space of forty days, we are asked to return to the Lord with fasting, prayer, and acts of love. But even more deeply, we are called to justice—to a conversion that transforms not only our individual lives, but our relationships, our communities, and the very structures of the world around us.

The words of the prophet Isaiah pierce the soul with clarity and hope. They challenge us: *"Wash yourselves, make yourselves clean. Cease to do evil. Learn to do good."* And they comfort us: *"Though your sins are like scarlet, they shall be as white as snow."* Here we see Lent not as a season of shame, but as an invitation from a loving God who desires to reason with us, to draw us back, to renew and restore us.

Isaiah's prophetic voice echoes the demand of the Gospel—a demand not rooted in legalism or fear, but in love and justice. Lent is not simply about giving things up. It is about making room for God's reign. It is about remembering the poor, lifting-up the oppressed, caring for the vulnerable, and pleading for those who have no voice. The spirituality of Lent, therefore, is not just personal; it is radically communal. It is a summons to action.

In the American National Catholic Church, we recognize the Gospel's insistent call to be a people of compassion, integrity, and inclusion. The prophet's call to "search for justice, help the oppressed, be just to the orphan, plead for the widow" resonates powerfully with our mission. Our Eucharistic life cannot be separated from our commitment to justice. Our worship must lead us to service, and our prayer must empower us for solidarity.

This Lent, I invite all our parishes, communities, and individual faithful to deepen our Lenten journey by embracing a spirituality that is rooted in both contemplation and justice. Let our fasting create space for the hungry. Let our prayer expand our hearts for the suffering. Let our almsgiving become a sign of our solidarity with the poor.

Let us also remember that we do not undertake this journey alone. The Lord walks with us. The same God who calls us to repentance is the One who promises renewal: *"Come now, let us talk this over... though your sins are like scarlet, they shall be as white as snow."* In Christ, there is no condemnation, only the invitation to be made new.

We are companions on this journey, and this Lent, I invite you to deepen your spiritual experience by praying with us through our ANCC Lenten Retreat reflections provided by our clergy and seminarians. Listen as the ANCC invites us to reflect on the Gospels of Lent with our American National Catholic Women Speak, and to engage the dimensions of our faith with the ANCC's Podcast, Renewing the Spirit.

To the clergy of our Church, I urge you to preach boldly the prophetic Gospel of Lent. Offer the sacrament of reconciliation as a place not of fear, but of healing. Let our liturgies in this season reflect the depth of God's mercy and the breadth of God's justice.

To all the People of God, I pray that this Lent may be for you a time of grace, transformation, and profound encounter with Christ. May our Lenten practices form us more fully into the likeness of Jesus, who gave himself for the life of the world.

And may we emerge from these forty days as a Church renewed in mission, reconciled in heart, and recommitted to justice.

With every blessing for the journey ahead,

+ George R. Lucey, FCM

Most Rev. George R. Lucey, FCM
Presiding Bishop

November 27 2024

A Thanksgiving Letter from the Presiding Bishop of the American National Catholic Church

In the name of the Father and of the +Son, and of the Holy Spirit.

To the People of God, Seminarians, Inquirers, and Clergy of the American National Catholic Church,

Grace and peace to you from God our Father and the Lord Jesus Christ.

As we gather in this season of Thanksgiving, I write to you with a heart full of gratitude for your unwavering dedication to proclaiming the extravagant and inclusive love of God through Jesus Christ. Truly, as St. Paul proclaimed, "Thanks be to God for His indescribable gift" (*2 Corinthians 9:15*). The gift of finding each other in a community of faith dedicated to witnessing to the values of the Kingdom.

Each of you—whether you serve as clergy, are discerning a call to ministry, or live out your faith as laity—plays an integral role in the mission of the ANCC. Your prayers, service, and support have been invaluable in making our Church a beacon of God's love and compassion in the world. Through your commitment, you embody the call to love one another and extend Christ's welcome to all into the experience of God's love at the heart of our Catholic faith.

On this Thanksgiving Day, let us join together in a spirit of profound gratitude for the many blessings God has bestowed upon us: the gift of our faith, the bonds of our community, and the privilege to serve as St. Teresa of Avila reminds us, as His hands and feet in the world.

I invite you to celebrate this gratitude with us by joining our Thanksgiving Mass on Thursday, November 28 at 10:00 A.M. at the Cathedral Parish of St. Francis of Assisi. The service will be livestreamed on www.Facebook.com/stfrancisnj. Together, let us offer our thanks and consecrate this day to God with prayer and joy.

Let us also reflect on the inspiring words of St. Mary Euphrasia Pelletier, who reminds us that, "Gratitude is the memory of the heart." May this truth guide us as we remember and cherish the graces we have received. May this gratitude which inflames our hearts help us to persevere in generous service to all we meet.

Let us pray:

Father in Heaven, Creator of all and source of all goodness and love,

Please look kindly upon us and receive our heartfelt gratitude in this time of giving thanks.

Thank you for all the graces and blessings You have bestowed upon us, both spiritual and temporal: our faith and religious heritage, our food and shelter, our health, the love we share with one another, and the gift of our family and friends.

Dear Father, in Your infinite generosity, please grant us continued graces and blessings throughout the coming year.

This we ask in the Name of Jesus, Your Son and our Brother. Amen.

May the peace of Christ fill your hearts this Thanksgiving, and may our shared gratitude strengthen our bond as the Body of Christ.

With every blessing,

Most Rev. George R. Lucey, FCM

Presiding Bishop

The American National Catholic Church

June 2 2024

So, then you are no longer strangers and aliens, but you are fellow citizens with the saints and members of the household of God, built on the foundation of the apostles and prophets, Christ Jesus himself being the cornerstone, in whom the whole structure, being joined together, grows into a holy temple in the Lord. In him you also are being built together into a dwelling place for God by the Spirit.
- Ephesians 2:19–22

Dear Sisters and Brothers,

Peace!

We in the American National Catholic Church, who draw on our shared faith and experience, note with some care for all of you who might be members of the parish communities which are closing or consolidating in the Archdiocese of Baltimore.

The American National Catholic Church suspects that this was a very difficult decision on the part of the administration of the Archdiocese and prays for all involved.

For all of us as Catholics, our parish is our spiritual home. It is where the seeds of faith, hope, and love take root in us and are continually nourished through the sacramental life of the Church. As Catholics, our entire life is lived up and down the aisle of our parish home. We were carried down the aisle at our Baptism, walked down the aisle to experience Reconciliation, and with awe and wonder walked the same aisle to receive the Body and Blood of Christ. At Confirmation, we confidently marched down our parish aisle, eager to reaffirm our faith. With joy and hope for the future, we walked the aisle on Wedding days and ordinations. At the end of our lives, we are again carried down the very same parish aisle, one last time. Our parishes are the locus where we experience and share in the joys and sorrows of our community life with others who share our love for God and one another in our faith Traditions.

We know the tremendous loss to the spiritual and communal quality of our lives as our parishes close, and we want you to know of the parish community of Our Lady Undoer of Knots American National Catholic Parish, located in the greater Baltimore area at Edmondson Ave in West Baltimore, MD (https://our-lady-undoer-of-knots.org) and Nuestra Senora de la Medalla Milagrosa American National Catholic Parish located in Germantown, MD (https://rb.gy/llxftm). Please know you are welcome to join us in the celebration of the extravagant love of God at the heart of the Church, lived out in our all-inclusive Catholic parishes.

Please be assured also of our prayers for you and our hope that you might find a home with us as we journey together to witness to the Kingdom in our midst.

20 August 2018

A Pastoral Letter from the Presiding Bishop George Lucey, FCM

on the clergy abuses in Roman Catholic dioceses in Pennsylvania

In the name + of the Father, Son, and Holy Spirit!

Last week brought yet another horrific revelation of the sexual, psychological, and physical abuse of children perpetrated by spiritually unworthy Roman Catholic priests and covered up by timid bishops. A grand jury report, in the making for two years, disclosed that over 1,000 children in six Pennsylvania dioceses had been molested by 300 priests over a seventy-year span. The grand jury concluded that there were likely many more cases of abuse that were never reported or never recorded.

Along with people of good will everywhere, and especially in solidarity with the victims of abuse and their families, I wish to express my shock and grief at this latest disclosure of the unspeakable damage clerical secrecy and ecclesial hierarchy can inflict upon Christ's church. The sins of the abusers and the bishops who did little or nothing to stop them brings to mind the prophet Habakkuk's rebuke: "The very stones in the walls cry out against you, and the beams in the ceilings echo the complaint." (Hab 2:11)

I am mindful that all of us fall short of who God wishes us to be, that all of us one day will stand before the heavenly judgment seat to answer for our sins, that all of us hope that on that day God's justice will be tempered with mercy, and that we therefore are likewise called to do the same when responding to the sins of our brothers and sisters. But I'm also mindful that the Lord commanded us on numerous occasions to be especially protective of those in our midst who are the most vulnerable: the poor, socially marginalized, disabled, and adrift. Surely innocent children top that list.

Accordingly, the people of the American National Catholic Church join their voices to that of their sorrowful Roman Catholic sisters and brothers in calling for a full accounting of clerical abuse, an open-hearted and good faith rethinking of protocols and procedures for dealing with it, and a sincere examination of the ways in which ecclesial secrecy and hierarchy in the Roman communion has contributed to so much child abuse.

Inspired and led by the Holy Spirit, the American National Catholic Church has from its very inception offered itself as a place of refuge for the oppressed as well as a healing place for those who may have been betrayed and wounded by unworthy pastors or oppressive religious institutions. We take as our own St.

Francis of Assisi's calling to rebuild God's church in order, as he said, "to heal wounds, to unite what has fallen apart, and to bring home those who have lost their way." Consequently, we sincerely welcome with compassion and love all who feel spiritually orphaned by this or past revelations of clerical abuse in the Roman Catholic Church, just as we continue to offer prayers for that communion's healing.

Given on the Memorial of St. Bernard of Clairvaux

Most Rev. George R. Lucey, FCM

Presiding Bishop

The American National Catholic Church

May 5, 2017

A Pastoral Letter From Ancc Presiding Bishop George R. Lucey, Fcm For

The Fourth Sunday Of Easter – Good Shepherd (Vocations) Sunday

+ In the name of the Father, and of the Son, and of the Holy Spirit!

Traditionally, the fourth Sunday of Easter, "Good Shepherd Sunday," is an occasion to remind the faithful of the importance of vocation. Accordingly, I invite all persons in the American National Catholic Church (ANCC) to pray that God might help them fulfill the vocation to which God calls them. As Vatican Council-II reminded us, the fostering of vocations is a task of the entire Christian community, exercised above all by the cultivation of a fully Christian life.

Participation in the community's fostering of vocations can lead some to think and pray about the possibility of ordained ministry. Therefore, the ANCC invites women and men to consider prayerfully if God is calling you to ordained service in the Church.

God invites each of to "go out into the deep." Doing so, as St. Peter and the Apostles discovered, always requires trust, courage, and commitment. Serving God as a priest or deacon in the ANCC especially calls forth these three virtues. Because we are a young and small jurisdiction, following Christ in ordained ministry often must be done without the institutional support of a larger ecclesial body.

Yet the rewards are immense. Precisely because we are small, persons called to ordained ministry have the blessed opportunities to plant parishes from the ground up by seeking out those who hunger, sometimes desperately, for a spiritual home that will welcome them just as they are. There is a spiritual excitement, a sense of holy adventure, which animates ministry in the ANCC, not dissimilar, surely, to the Holy Spirit-inspired exhilaration that the earliest Christians must have felt.

We know from requests for information we receive every week that there is a great longing throughout the nation for more ANCC parishes. As a small jurisdiction, we cannot hope to plant new parishes without dedicated people eager to honor the vocations, ordained or otherwise, to which God calls them. I ask you to pray about how you can use your gifts and talents to build up the jurisdiction, plant new parishes, and continue to witness to the central truth of the inclusive and extravagant love of God at the heart of the Church Catholic.

+ George R. Lucey, FCM

Most Rev. George R. Lucey, FCM

Presiding Bishop

August 20, 2013

Dear sisters and brothers of the American National Catholic Church,

Peace and apostolic blessings! I wanted to capture some of my thoughts of our first clergy convocation and share them with you as we continue together to discern where the Holy Spirit is leading us.

First, let me thank each and every one of you for making the time to attend our first convocation. Your attendance required personal sacrifice and speaks to me of your commitment to dedicating the time and energy needed to establish the ANCC as a credible and valid expression of Catholicism in the United States. Thank you all.

My first impression is formed by this tremendous dedication to the mission of the ANCC. What follows from this dedication, I think is, a feeling of confidence in who we minister with. I heard what several of the members of the gathering captured - the sense of safety we feel in ministering in the ANCC. We are able to say this because we have established a set of criteria which all members of the clergy must meet before anyone can minister in the church. This assurance of a professional and fair process is a logical outgrowth of the founding principle of the ANCC to capture the promise of the Independent Sacramental Movement (ISM) movement, while learning from and avoiding the mistakes made by others so many times before. The ANCC's adherence to this founding principle has created a presbyterate in which we can have a sense of trust in those we ministering alongside.

Many of our discussions about the Church led us back to the Eucharist. Indeed our entire gathering was very much centered on our time at the Eucharist. I witnessed how all us of see ourselves as Catholics gathered around the gift of God's self in the Eucharist. Many of us - in fact most of us - echoed the Second Vatican Council's belief about the life of the Church flowing from the Eucharist. We seemed to embody the Council's view of the Eucharist as essentially in the people of God, the Body of Christ, and the importance of including everyone in our beliefs about communion. This reminded me about the importance of the life of prayer to us all and how that message organically flows to the people who we are sent to minister to. From this we recall that we have been called to preach the Gospel of Jesus Christ - not our own. In the midst of the grace flowing from our life of prayer, centered around the Eucharist, we saw how we had to unite ourselves to the missio dei.

From this sense of dedication, trust, creative energy, and understanding ourselves as a Eucharistic Church, grew the sense of safety to explore ourselves in a missional dimension. We continue to experience the joy of rediscovering the importance of God's call to be God's people and exploring what it means to be Jesus' presence in the world. We realized that we are not bound by the institutional constraints of others. As a result we can form communities striving to live out Christ's command to love each other as he loved us.

My prayer is that we will be able to harness the tremendous creative energy I felt in the members of the convocation. As I listened to many of you share what attracted you to the ANCC, I heard the joy of being able to minister in the manner we have heard God calling. Each of us has found here some expression of the truest desires of our hearts being fulfilled. I saw the joy of discovering a priesthood more concerned with the Church communicating the love of God to everyone than with finding a way to fence off God's grace. This energy is diverse, and I am not naïve enough to think that we all agree with each other on every aspect of the Church's future; however, I think the convocation provided a forum where everyone felt that their voice could be heard and respected. Now, the task for us is to organize this energy into a common vision, engaging everyone's unique talents.

Sincerely yours in Christ,

Most Rev. George R. Lucey, FCM
Presiding Bishop

Preamble Statement by George R. Lucey, FCM, Presiding Bishop of The

American National Catholic Church

October 4, 2009

American National Catholic Church

Code of Canon Law

Preamble

We wish you grace and peace in the name of the Father, and of the Son, and of the Holy Spirit.

We the people of God, in this year of grace 2009, having prayed to God for guidance from the Holy Spirit feel called in this place and time to organize the American National Catholic Church as a living witness to the Spirit of God who renews God's Church in every age. We declare that we are a valid expression of the ancient Catholic faith, theologically, sacramentally, and pastorally rooted to the One, Holy, Catholic, and Apostolic Church which flowed from the side of Jesus Christ as he hung upon the cross. We affirm that we are born of the same Holy Spirit which inspired the Apostles on Pentecost with courage to proclaim in every tongue the all---embracing love of God at the heart of our Incarnational experience of God ever present in our world.

We celebrate the unity of the Catholic Church even in her diverse expressions and offer ourselves as a valid Church within the ancient Catholic Tradition, laying claim to the truth of the foundational creeds of the Catholic Church. Further we find an articulation for the American National Catholic Church in the words of Lumen Gentium, the Dogmatic Constitution on the Church from that wonderful moment in history when the Church was inspired by the spirit of Pentecost to declare:

> In virtue of this catholicity each individual part of the Church contributes through its special gifts to the good of the other parts and of the whole Church. Thus through the common sharing of gifts and through the common effort to attain fullness in unity, the whole and each of the parts receive increase. Not only, then, is the People of God made up of different peoples, but even in its inner structure it is composed of various ranks. This diversity among its members arises either by reason of their duties as is the case with those who exercise the

> sacred ministry for the good of their brethren, or by
> reason of their situation and way of life, as is the case
> with those many who enter the religious state and,
> tending toward holiness by a narrower path, stimulate
> their brethren by their example.
>
> Moreover, within the Church particular Churches hold
> their rightful place. These Churches retain their own
> Traditions without in any way lessening the primacy of
> the Chair of Peter. . .
>
> Finally, between all the parts of the Church there
> remains a bond of close communion with respect to
> spiritual riches, apostolic workers, and temporal
> resources. For the members of the People of God are
> called to share these goods, and to each of the Churches
> the words of the Apostle apply: "According to the gift
> each has received, administer it to one another as good
> stewards of the manifold grace of God" (1Peter 4:10).[5]

Reflecting on the current state of Church in the world, we feel called by God's loving Son to Incarnate anew, in the American National Catholic Church this unifying, liberating, and renewing Spirit of God in an attempt to stimulate our brethren and ourselves to the holiness and wholeness we are all called to by the extravagant example of God's love made manifest in the Paschal Mystery of our Savior Jesus Christ.

Thus we pray that the Canons of the American National Catholic Church will reflect our commitment to spreading the all--- inclusive love of God, by providing a liberating set of norms to govern our Church with Christ as our model for charity and his Holy Mother Mary as our model for humility.

Blessings,

The Most Rev. George R. Lucey, FCM

First Presiding Bishop of the American National Catholic Church

October 4, 2009

---

[5] Abbott, Walter M, S.J., Ed. (1966) The Documents of Vatican II. Herder and Herder: New York, page 31-32

Discussion Questions

1. How do these letters reflect *Lumen Gentium*'s vision of the Church as communion rather than hierarchy alone?

2. In what ways is authority exercised pastorally rather than juridically in these texts?

3. How do the letters addressing ecclesial failure (e.g., abuse) contribute to, rather than undermine, the Church's holiness?

4. What role does baptismal dignity play in shaping the ANCC's understanding of ministry and co-responsibility?

6. How might these letters challenge clericalism within broader Catholic contexts?

Chapter III: Ecumenism and Interreligious Dialogue

(Unitatis Redintegratio & Nostra Aetate)

Introduction to the Letters in This Category

The pastoral letters in this category give concrete expression to the Second Vatican Council's conviction that the search for unity is intrinsic to the Church's faithfulness to Christ. Unitatis Redintegratio and Nostra Aetate together articulate a Catholicism no longer defined by opposition, but by dialogue, mutual respect, and shared witness to truth.

These letters—addressed to Popes, Orthodox leaders, Protestant bishops, and other Christian communities—are not mere diplomatic gestures. They are theological statements affirming that the Holy Spirit is at work beyond the visible boundaries of any single ecclesial structure. By acknowledging shared baptism, common Scripture, and genuine holiness in other traditions, the ANCC situates itself firmly within the Council's renewed understanding of Catholicity.

The inclusion of these letters together reflects an ecclesial humility that recognizes division as a wound in the Body of Christ. Dialogue here is not pursued for strategic advantage or institutional validation, but as an act of obedience to Christ's prayer "that they may all be one" (John 17:21). Such dialogue is understood as both a gift and a discipline, requiring patience, truthfulness, and charity.

Readers are invited to receive these texts as part of the ANCC's broader commitment to being a Church of bridges rather than barriers—a community confident enough in its Catholic identity to encounter others without fear, trusting that unity grows not through coercion but through love lived in truth.

May 8 2025

A Letter of Congratulations to His Holiness, Pope Leo XIV

May it please Your Holiness,

Grace and peace to you in the name of our Lord and Savior, Jesus Christ.

On behalf of the American National Catholic Church, I extend our heartfelt congratulations and fraternal greetings upon your election as Bishop of Rome and Supreme Pontiff of the Catholic Church. We honor the Petrine ministry entrusted to you and pray that your pontificate may be filled with wisdom, compassion, and an ever-deepening commitment to the Gospel of Jesus Christ.

We in the American National Catholic Church hold the office of the papacy in deep respect, recognizing it as a visible sign of unity and service within the Church Catholic. While we walk parallel paths in faith and mission, we remain joined by our shared commitment to the teachings and love of Christ.

In the Gospel according to Luke, we read:

> *"Master," said John, "we saw someone driving out demons in your name and we tried to stop him, because he is not one of us." "Do not stop him," Jesus said, "for whoever is not against you is for you."*

> — Luke 9:49–50

These words remind us that the mission of Christ transcends institutional boundaries and invites all who labor in His name to a spirit of mutual recognition and fraternal charity.

May the Holy Spirit guide your ministry and may your witness continue to be a beacon of hope, justice, and reconciliation in our world. Be assured of our prayers for you and for the Church entrusted to your care.

In the peace of Christ,

Most Rev. George R. Lucey, FCM

Presiding Bishop

A Letter to Pope Francis from the Presiding Bishop of the ANCC

January 3, 2025
His Holiness Pope Francis
Your Holiness,

Grace and peace to you in the name of our Lord Jesus Christ. I write to you as Bishop George Lucey, the Presiding Bishop of the American National Catholic Church (ANCC), to express heartfelt gratitude for your courageous leadership of the Church. Your unwavering commitment to the Gospel and your dedication to the vision of a Church that truly embodies mercy, justice, and inclusivity continue to inspire countless faithful around the world.

The American National Catholic Church is a Catholic jurisdiction that finds its identity and mission deeply rooted in the Spirit of the Second Vatican Council. We embrace its call for renewal and reform with profound joy, and we are committed to living out its vision of a Church that engages the modern world with compassion and hope. Our parishes and ministries are vibrant communities where the reforms of Vatican II are lived without tension, and where the people of God find a welcoming and affirming home.

In our sacramental life, pastoral outreach, and commitment to social justice, we seek to reflect the Church as envisioned by the Council: a Church that is truly the People of God, journeying together in faith, responding to the signs of the times, and proclaiming the Good News to all. We are particularly inspired by your emphasis on synodality, dialogue, and the preferential option for the poor, values that resonate deeply within our community.

Your Holiness, we recognize the challenges and opposition you have faced in your efforts to lead the Church into a deeper fidelity to its mission. Please know that you are not alone in this work. We stand in solidarity with you, and we pray daily for your strength, wisdom, and health as you continue to shepherd the Church with courage and humility.

As you guide the universal Church in its ongoing discernment and reform, we remain steadfast in our support and in our commitment to living out the Catholic faith in ways that honor the Gospel and serve the common good. May the Holy Spirit continue to inspire and sustain you in your ministry, and may God bless you abundantly.

In Christ's peace,

Most Rev. George R. Lucey, FCM
Presiding Bishop
American National Catholic Church

CC: Monsignor Leonardo Sapienza
        Regent of the Prefecture of the Papal Household
        Apostolic Palace 00120 Vatican City

June 17 2016

Presiding Bishop sends his greetings to the Orthodox Church as they prepare for their Holy and Great Council

Greetings to My Orthodox Brothers in Christ!

I send joyful and fraternal greetings to you as you prepare for the Holy and Great Council of the Orthodox Church in discernment of where the Spirit would have you go.

We live in troubled times. But as children of the Resurrected God, we know that grief is always accompanied by hope, because the Kingdom is in our midst, in the here-and-now, if we but have eyes to see it and hearts to embrace it.

As the Vatican-II document Unitatis redintegratio (Article 17) notes, Orthodoxy and Catholicism have much in common spiritually, theologically, and liturgically. Despite our historical differences, we are joined together as branches of the One Vine. May we enter ever more deeply into fellowship with one another as members of the united and undivided Body of Christ.

On behalf of the People of God in the American National Catholic Church, I wish you a fruitful Council. You will be in my prayers.

Given under my hand and seal, the 17th day of June in the Year of Our Lord 2016 on the Feasts of Martyr Nectan of Hartland (Orthodox) and St. Albert Chmielowski (Latin).

Yours In Christ,

Most Reverend George R. Lucey, FCM

Presiding Bishop

July 1 2015

Feast of St. Oliver Plunkett

Dear Presiding Bishop--- elect Curry:

On behalf of the people of God and the clergy of the American National Catholic Church (ANCC), I send you fraternal greetings and congratulations as you prepare to shepherd the Episcopal Church in America. The overwhelming number of bishops and delegates who voted for you at General Convention truly attests to the presence and guidance of the Holy Spirit.

We in the ANCC have a deep affection for the Episcopal Church. Several of our parishes enjoy cordial relations with nearby Episcopal ones, and one of our clergy was actually an Episcopal deacon before incardinating with us.

All of us in the ANCC are grateful for the courage of the Episcopal Church in general, and yours in particular, in taking the lead on important social issues and thereby expanding the range of Catholic theological praxis. As an independent Catholic jurisdiction with parishes in North Dakota, New Mexico, Missouri, Florida, Virginia, Pennsylvania, New Jersey, and Connecticut, we have much in common, in theology as well as mission, with our Episcopal sisters and brothers.

Please know that you are in my prayers as you prepare to serve as Presiding Bishop of the Episcopal Church in America. I look forward to meeting you, when things settle down a bit for you, to share a meal and fellowship. I'm just across the river from New York City.

In the meantime, I remain.

Yours in Christ,

Most Reverend George R. Lucey, FCM

Presiding Bishop

The American National Catholic Church

October 7 2019

An Open Letter to His Holiness Pope Francis

Memorial of Our Lady of the Rosary

Your Holiness:

As Presiding Bishop of the American National Catholic Church (ANCC), it's been on my mind and heart in recent months to write to you. I have two reasons for doing so.

The first is to convey my heartfelt regret at the continued assaults you've endured from conservative critics within your communion. Their criticism stems from their vehement dislike of your efforts to shepherd the Roman Catholic Church in the spirit of the Vatican Council-II. The most recent example of their animosity was on full display in July at the Napa Institute when Cardinal Raymond Burke, George Weigel, and others claimed that under your leadership the Roman Church has fallen into serious doctrinal and moral error.

I humbly encourage you to continue with the mission you've undertaken as pope to remind the Roman Church of what's truly important in the service of Our Lord.

My second reason for writing you is to affirm that the jurisdiction over which I preside is bringing to fruition the dream I believe you have for the Catholic tradition we both love. Inspired by Vatican II's vision of what the Body of Christ is called to be, the ANCC upholds the social justice principles of subsidiarity and solidarity, practices a polity that avoids top-down authoritarianism and encourages synodality, and strives to evangelize in the spirit of humility, charity, and inclusivity.

Fifty years ago, Saint John XXIII threw open the windows of the Roman Church to let in the fresh air of the twentieth century. I applaud your efforts to reopen those windows in the twenty-first century. Please pray for me, as I will pray for you, that both of us may continue, each in our own jurisdictions, to uphold with integrity, creativity, and gratitude Vatican II's vision of what the Church might be.

I remain your brother in Christ,

Most Reverend George R. Lucey, FCM

Presiding Bishop

March 18, 2015

Bishop George Lucey's Response to Fr. Anthony Lipari's Laicization

Recently the Archdiocese of Newark published an article about Fr. Anthony Lipari's laicization, which appeared on the Archdiocese of Newark's webpage. Bishop O'Connell of the Trenton Diocese followed suite and re-published the article in the Trenton Diocese. Now I understand that Archbishop Myers has ordered the article to be published in the bulletins of the parishes where Fr. Anthony had served.

I was struck by both its mean-spirited tone and its misrepresentation of the facts. It is patently untrue that Fr. Anthony abandoned the Roman Catholic Church. He was asked to leave by Archbishop Myer's Vicar General, despite the fact that his record in the Archdiocese was stellar.

In accord with Catholic teaching on the ontological character of his ordination, Fr. Anthony has continued his priesthood in the American National Catholic Church in order to honor his vocation to serve the People of God.

So the supercilious and hurtful tone of the Archbishop's announcement about Fr. Anthony slanders a good priest. But more to the point, such untrue and slanderous public statements have negative consequences for the American National Catholic Church in the United States. As you well know, the Roman Catholic Church has no authority in the United States to determine who and who cannot call themselves Catholic. The word "Catholic" is not Rome's exclusive property.

On a personal note, I think the prominent placement of the notice of Fr. Anthony's laicization on the webpage of the Archdiocese is meant to imply that Fr. Anthony poses some threat to the Roman Catholics of the Archdiocese. My pastoral education taught me that such matters are properly handled using the internal forum rather than public forum. For the Archbishop to publicly announce a laicization in order to insinuate that Fr. Anthony is a threat to Roman Catholic laity is surprising at best and the least Christ-like action he could have taken.

We believe the American National Catholic Church was called into being by the Holy Spirit. We neither are nor wish to be in opposition to the Roman Catholic Church. Yet Archbishop Myers and Bishop O'Connell of the Trenton diocese have on several occasions very publicly pronounced our priests and sacraments to be invalid. I doubt that these two prelates would publish the same about Episcopalian, Methodist, Coptic, or Polish National Catholic clergy.

Given the continuous scandal of Archbishop Myers extravagant spending on his personal residence, the less than transparent manner in which he addressed the sexual abuse of children in the archdiocese with the Michael Fugee case, the

People of God would be justified in having more doubt about the validity of Orders in the Roman Catholic Church than in the American National Catholic Church.

Ironically, the churlishness of public comments by Roman Catholic prelates only further damages the already poor perception of the Roman Catholic Church in Newark, serving to drive many former Roman Catholics into the arms of the American National Catholic Church. As the old adage goes, "there is no such thing as negative press," and the ANCC continues to reap the benefits of these unhappy public attempts at power and control.

Yours In Christ,

Most Reverend George R. Lucey, FCM
Presiding Bishop

Discussion Questions

1. How do these letters articulate Catholic identity while remaining genuinely open to other Christian traditions?

2. What theological assumptions make ecumenical dialogue possible without relativism?

3. How does Vatican II's understanding of "elements of sanctification and truth" shape the tone of these letters?

4. In what ways is dialogue presented as a spiritual discipline rather than a strategic tool?

5. What implications do these letters have for the Church's credibility in a religiously plural world?

Chapter IV: Dignity of the Human Person and Inclusion

(Dignitatis Humanae)

SAINT
OF
MARY
EGYPT

Introduction to the Letters in This Category

The letters gathered in this section are anchored in the Church's unwavering affirmation of the inherent dignity of every human person. Drawing on Dignitatis Humanae and the broader trajectory of Catholic Social Teaching, these texts address questions of conscience, freedom, identity, and belonging—particularly as they affect those who have experienced marginalization within Church and society.

Vatican II's teaching on religious freedom marked a decisive development in Catholic doctrine by affirming that truth cannot be imposed but must be freely embraced. The ANCC extends this principle pastorally, insisting that coercion—whether doctrinal, sacramental, or social—undermines both human dignity and the credibility of the Gospel. Letters addressing LGBTQ+ persons, women's voices, marriage equality, immigration, and gender identity belong together because they apply this conciliar insight to contemporary human realities.

These texts do not abandon Catholic moral reasoning; rather, they situate it within a relational and incarnational framework shaped by conscience, accompaniment, and mercy. Influenced by modern moral theologians and by lived pastoral experience, they reflect a conviction that the development of doctrine must be guided by both fidelity to tradition and attentiveness to human suffering.

Read as a whole, this category articulates an ANCC vision of inclusion that is neither relativistic nor reactionary, but deeply Christological: grounded in the belief that every person is created in the image of God and called into communion. These letters invite the reader to consider inclusion not as a concession, but as conversion.

12 December 2025

PROCLAMATION AT MASS
Feast of Our Lady of Guadalupe

Dear brothers and sisters in Christ,

Dear holy people of God gathered under the maternal protection of Our Lady of Guadalupe:

In light of the Feast of Our Lady of Guadalupe, and in the midst of the horrors of the current injustices and the shameful immigration policies now affecting our Church community, I wish to extend my heartfelt greetings to you. As we honor Our Lady of Guadalupe—Patroness of all the Americas—we turn our hearts to her maternal protection and her unwavering solidarity with the poor, the vulnerable, and all who suffer. To every member of our community, especially those living in fear, uncertainty, or discrimination, I offer my pastoral concern, my prayers, and my steadfast commitment to stand with you in this difficult hour.

On this blessed feast day, I extend to you my Apostolic Blessings and my warmest and most heartfelt greetings. Today we look to the Virgin of Tepeyac, ever present among her people, interceding for us, protecting us, and guiding all who seek justice, dignity, and peace.

As your pastor, I must speak with you from the depths of my heart. Our communities are suffering under unjust and arbitrary policies, and the harsh and often dehumanizing actions carried out by ICE. These actions have created fear, instability, and profound pain within many of our families. None of us remains untouched by these dark practices that obscure the face of mercy and stand in contradiction to the Gospel we proclaim.

Just as our ancestors in faith endured persecution and violence from the powerful and yet remained steadfast in hope, we too find ourselves in a time of trial. But your courage, your fidelity, and your unwavering witness strengthen my own faith. You refuse to allow anything or anyone to take away what is essential: your dignity, your faith, and your identity as beloved children of God. This, dear people of God, is a shining testimony to the whole Church.

Today I unite my prayers with yours, imploring the Lord for a swift end to all forms of discrimination, racism, and abuse of power. May this nation once a beacon promising peace, safety, and the possibility of a flourishing life turn again toward justice and compassion.

May Our Lady of Guadalupe wrap you in her tilma of love, sustain you in hope, and lead us all along the path of peace and justice.

Remain strong and courageous. Know that you are held in my heart and in my prayers, and that the boundless grace of God accompanies you always.

With my Apostolic Blessing,

Most Rev. George R. Lucey, FCM
Presiding Bishop

9 March 2025

American National Catholic Women Speak: Elevating Women's Voices in the Church

The American National Catholic Church (ANCC) is proud to announce the launch of American National Catholic Women Speak, a transformative initiative dedicated to amplifying the voices and contributions of women in the Church. This effort is part of the ANCC's ongoing commitment to the New Evangelization, fostering inclusivity and empowering women to share their experiences, wisdom, and faith in meaningful ways.

Through this initiative, women from diverse backgrounds within the ANCC will have a platform to engage in dialogue, reflect on their spiritual journeys, and contribute to the Church's mission of justice, love, and service. American National Catholic Women Speak recognizes the vital role women have played throughout Christian history and seeks to ensure their voices continue to shape the future of the Church.

The platform will feature reflections on the readings from the lectionary, providing deeper insights into Scripture and its relevance in contemporary life. By providing a space for women to share their perspectives, the ANCC hopes to foster a richer and more inclusive ecclesial community.

For more information, visit anccwomenspeak.wordpress.com.

The American National Catholic Church is an inclusive Catholic community, independent of the Roman Catholic Church, dedicated to making the world a more caring place. Guided by a presiding bishop, the ANCC celebrates the same sacraments as the Roman Church and follows the spirit of reform initiated by the Second Vatican Council. Although sharing core theological and liturgical practices with Roman Catholicism, the ANCC differs on several major points, such as married clergy, female priests, divorce and re-marriage, same-sex marriage, and lay leadership. The Church has parishes across the U.S. and a host of ministries to the alienated, under-served, and forgotten. For more information, visit www.TheANCC.org.

January 20, 2025

Memorial of Saint Sebastian, Martyr

"You shall not pervert the justice due to the sojourner or to the fatherless, or take a widow's garment in pledge, but you shall remember that you were a slave in Egypt and the LORD your God redeemed you from there; therefore I command you to do this"
(Deuteronomy 24:17-18).

Dear Sisters and Brothers in Christ,

In the name of the Father, and of the Son+ and of the Holy Spirit.

Grace and peace to you from God our Creator, the Redeemer who walks with us, and the Holy Spirit who empowers us to live as agents of divine love in the world.

As we journey together in this sacred season of Ordinary Time, a season of hope and renewal, I write to you on this Inauguration Day, a pastoral declaration of our commitment as a Catholic jurisdiction to mercy, justice and compassion and a promise to continue commitment as members of the American National Catholic Church to embody the boundless love of God. In a world often fractured by division and exclusion, we are called to be a living sign of God's radical inclusion, rooted in the mysteries of our Catholic faith and expressed through our unwavering commitment to the marginalized and stigmatized.

The Extravagant Love of God

At the heart of our faith is the unshakable truth that God's love is extravagant and unconditional. This love was made manifest in the incarnation, passion, death, and resurrection of Jesus Christ, who embraced all, especially those deemed unworthy by societal standards. As followers of Christ, we are invited to mirror this love—a love that sees the dignity and worth of every human being, created in the image of God.

Our commitment to radical inclusion flows from this foundational truth. It is not merely an ideal but a lived reality that compels us to welcome all who seek God's grace, regardless of race, gender, sexual orientation, economic status, or life circumstances. In our parishes, ministries, and daily encounters, we are called to create spaces where all can encounter the liberating and healing presence of Christ.

A Church for the Marginalized and Stigmatized

The Gospel repeatedly shows us Jesus special concern for those on the margins—the poor, the outcast, the sinner, and the forgotten. In this, we find our mission: to stand in solidarity with those who have been pushed to the edges of society, offering not judgment but compassion, not exclusion but embrace.

As a Church, we recommit ourselves to walking alongside those who have been wounded by prejudice, rejected by religious institutions, or left voiceless by systemic injustice. This includes our LGBTQ+ siblings, immigrants and refugees, those experiencing homelessness, and all who suffer from discrimination and exclusion. May our words and actions proclaim to them the Good News: that they are beloved, valued, and welcomed in the household of God.

The Dignity and Worth of Women

Central to our witness as the American National Catholic Church is our affirmation of the equal dignity and worth of women. We recognize the invaluable contributions of women to the life of the Church and the world, and we stand firmly against any structures or attitudes that diminish their God-given gifts.

In our commitment to justice and equality, we affirm the call of women to all levels of ministry and leadership within the Church. Their voices, perspectives, and gifts are not ancillary but essential to the flourishing of the Body of Christ. Let us continue to nurture communities where women's leadership is celebrated, and their prophetic witness is heeded.

Our Shared Journey

As we move forward together, let us hold fast to the values that define us as a Church: radical inclusion, compassion for the marginalized, and a steadfast commitment to justice and equality. These are not mere aspirations but the tangible ways we live out our faith in the God who has first loved us.

May our hearts be ever open to the movement of the Holy Spirit, who calls us to deeper love, greater courage, and unwavering hope. Let us continue to build communities that shine as beacons of God's extravagant love in a world yearning for healing and reconciliation.

With every blessing,

Most Rev. George R. Lucey, FCM
Presiding Bishop
The American National Catholic Church

Memorial of St. Lucy

December 13, 2022

> *But let justice roll down like waters, and righteousness like an ever-flowing stream. - Amos 5:24*

Today, with the signing of the Respect for Marriage Act, we in the American National Catholic Church can rejoice that we have come a little closer to the proposition that all people are created equal. The American National Catholic Church teaches, with the Church Catholic, that we are all created in the Image of God, and by virtue of that divine image each person is endowed with an intrinsic human dignity. What flows from this foundational understanding of the nature of our humanity is an invitation for all people to participate fully and safely in the Church and society.

The American National Catholic Church has intentionally interpreted the Church's teaching on the dignity of the human person as an implicit command of Christ to invite our LGBTQIA sisters and brothers into full participation in the sacramental life of the Church, along with all of those who enjoy inter-racial marriages. The legal protection given in the Respect for Marriage law aids the Christian community in moving toward the reality of justice for all.

June 17, 2020

Bishop George Lucey's response to the comments of Archbishop Jose Gomez regarding the Supreme Court's extending federal protection to LGBTQ

As Presiding Bishop of the American National Catholic Church, (www.TheANCC.org), I was unpleasantly surprised to read the comments by Archbishop Jose Gomez, President of the United States Conference of Catholic Bishops, criticizing and/or condemning the recent Supreme Court's decision on upholding Gay Rights and their acknowledgment of the rights of Gay people to full acceptance in the institutional life of American society. The Archbishop seems to be expressing a view contrary to the Catholic social teaching of Christ's preferential option for the poor and marginalized by suggesting that, as a Catholic prelate, he would exclude and condemn and marginalize gay/lesbian and transgender peoples.

The Archbishop in his comments expressed a view that could lead to our LGBTQ sister and brothers being seen as a threat rather than a gift to the Church, and equal members of the Body of Christ. His ideas contradict the Catholic Church's teaching on the radical inclusivity of Christ's command to love everyone as he loves us.

In fact in the lectionary for Mass during these weeks of ordinary times, we hear how Christ redefined love to go beyond the boundaries of prejudice and bias. As Christians and National Catholics, we strive to be inclusive as St. Paul instructs us. "In Christ, there are no social differences," (paraphrased).

I am reluctant, as an American National Catholic bishop to speak to the remarks by Archbishop Gomez of the Roman Catholic Church, and suspect that my voice will have little influence in inviting the Archbishop to remember as St. John tells us in his First Letter, "perfect love drives out all fear". There is nothing to be afraid of in lovingly embracing all of those who Christ embraces. We ask the Archbishop to come and pray with us at the American National Catholic Church to experience first hand, the love of Christ for ALL his people and the joy this brings to our congregants.

Most Rev. George R. Lucey, FCM

Presiding Bishop

13 June 2019

ANCC Responds to Vatican's Condemnation of Gender Fluidity

The American National Catholic Church (ANCC) is dismayed and disappointed at the release this week of a document from the Vatican's Congregation for Catholic Education, which condemns gender fluidity as "nothing more than a confused concept of freedom in the realm of feelings and wants."

The document, "'Male and Female He Created Them,'" claims that gender fluidity is "in direct contradiction of the model of marriage as being between one man and one woman, thereby destabilizing the family as an institution." The implication is that it falls into the "intrinsically disordered condition" category to which the Vatican has consigned same-sex attraction.

In saying this, the Vatican refuses to recognize that gender identity is a function of genetics and biochemistry, which sometimes are incompatible with anatomical structure. Consequently, the "feelings and wants" implicitly condemned are neither whimsical nor arbitrary. Nor can gender transition be written off "at the end of the day," as "only a 'provocative 'display against so-called 'traditional frameworks.'" It is instead an act of selfrecognition.

Sadly, the Vatican's condemnation provides, even if unintentionally, a rationalization for continuing discrimination against LGBTQ persons. The document urges readers to refrain from "bullying, violence, [and] insults." But in condemning gender fluidity as unnatural, confused, and sinfully rebellious, the covert message it communicates is quite different.

The American National Catholic Church celebrates each and every person as a beloved child of God. It affirms that the sacrament of marriage is intended to be available to all persons, regardless of their sexual orientation or gender identity, who are lovingly committed to one another. Such unions do not weaken or dishonor the sacrament. On the contrary, they affirm it as the consecrated covenant between two people who pledge their fidelity to one another before the God who made them as they are.

The American National Catholic Church is an inclusive Catholic community, independent of the Roman Catholic Church, dedicated to making the world a more caring place. Guided by a presiding bishop, the ANCC celebrates the same sacraments as the Roman Church and follows the spirit of reform initiated by the Second Vatican Council. Although sharing core theological and liturgical practices with Roman Catholicism, the ANCC differs on several major points, such as married clergy, female priests, divorce and re-marriage, same-sex marriage, and lay leadership. The Church has parishes across the U.S. and a host of ministries to the alienated, under-served, and forgotten. For more information, visit www.TheANCC.org.

21 December 2017

Thursday of the 3rd Week of Advent

A Pastoral Letter from Presiding Bishop George R. Lucey, FCM,

on Gender Identity

+ In the name of the Father, and of the Son, and of the Holy Spirit!

In mid-Advent, a season in which the faithful joyfully anticipate the birth of the Christ-child, the United States Council of Catholic Bishops (USCCB) released a letter praising "natural marriage"—that is, union between one man and one woman—and condemning transgender identity on the grounds that "human beings are male or female and that the socio-cultural reality of gender cannot be separated from one's sex as male or female." To presume otherwise, the letter states, "goes against reason" and is "deeply troubling."

The letter was co-signed by several representatives of non-Roman Catholic jurisdictions.

To its credit, the letter urged that Christians treat transgender persons "with compassion, mercy and honesty." But its insistence that "gender ideology" is a morally unworthy falsehood undercuts this counsel. To use the bishops' own language, the letter's message goes against reason and is deeply troubling.

There is a wealth of biological and psychological research, which affirms that "one's sex as male or female" in fact is not always compatible with gender identity, and that gender dysphoria is a genuine medical condition. We agree with the bishops that God created all humans with gender identity; but gender identity, we now know, may differ from sexual identity. Contrary to the bishops' claim, there is no rational basis for assuming that an acknowledgement of this calls God's design into question.

Moreover, the letter is deeply troubling from a pastoral, spiritual, and moral perspective, implying as it does that transgender persons are at best confused and at worst immoral. Especially disturbing is the letter's insistence that children who express a gender identity different from their sexual one are harmed if taken seriously by their parents and physicians. Caution is certainly appropriate in such cases, but not the blanket rejection urged by the bishops.

Throughout the centuries, the world has witnessed the tragic consequences that occur when the Church refuses to recognize the rich diversity of God's creation. In too many cases, entire groups of innocent people have been marginalized and even persecuted because they failed to conform to what the Church defined as normative or pleasing in the eyes of God.

Acknowledging this is not a denial that there are types of behavior, which are genuinely sinful. But new scientific and psychological discoveries about human sexuality and gender reveal that transgender identification is not one of them.

In the Vatican-II document on religious freedom entitled Dignitatis humanae, the Council fathers recognized that "a sense of the dignity of the human person has been impressing itself more and more deeply on the consciousness of contemporary persons." They affirmed that the Church should encourage humans to "act on their own judgment, enjoying and making use of a responsible freedom" in "the quest for the values proper to the human spirit."

The American National Catholic Church takes this affirmation seriously. Our human and all-too-finite understanding of God's will remains a work in progress. Although there is much in the Deposit of Faith that is certain and constant, our search for "values proper to the human spirit" continues. This isn't an endorsement of a laissez-faire "anything goes" attitude when it comes to morality. Rather, it's a humble and receptive openness to the ongoing work of the Holy Spirit, and a desire to enter ever more deeply into the loving kindness taught and exemplified by the Prince of Peace whose Nativity we will shortly celebrate.

Signed on this Thursday of the 3rd Week of Advent.

O Oriens, splendor lucis aeternae et sol iustitiae:

veni, et illumine sedentes in tenebris

et umbra mortis

Most Rev. George R. Lucey, FCM

Presiding Bishop

The American National Catholic Church

26 June 2017

A Pastoral Letter from Presiding Bishop George R. Lucey, FCM, on Roman Catholic Bishop Thomas Paprocki's Refusal of Christian Burial to Persons in Same-gender Relationships

+ In the name of the Father, and of the Son, and of the Holy Spirit!

Earlier this month, Thomas Paprocki, Roman Catholic bishop of Springfield, IL, issued a decree, ordering priests in his diocese to refuse communion and Christian burial to persons in same-gender relationships. Moreover, because such persons are deemed to be in "objectively immoral relationships," Bishop Paprocki proclaimed them ineligible to serve in any capacity in liturgical ministry, barred them as sponsors for either Baptism or Confirmation, and forbad them the Rite of Christian Initiation of Adults (RCIA).

This un-Christian directive deeply saddens me. I would like to respond to it from both a personal and pastoral perspective.

First, the personal.

In the second year of my priesthood I was asked to celebrate a Mass of Christian Burial for the partner of a man who had been in a loving and joyous same-gender relationship for over 20 years. His grieving widower shared with me that as a young adult, his partner had been in a Roman Catholic seminary for several years. But his growing awareness of his sexuality as well as his deep sense of integrity led him to leave the seminary and live openly as a gay man.

The widower told me that although his deceased partner loved the Church, he reached the point before his death where he could no longer abide the intolerance of his sexual identity he encountered at his local Roman Catholic parish. So he requested that his partner ask me to conduct the final rites of the Church in the Mass of Christian Burial. The funeral home was packed with friends and family of the deceased, many of whom were Catholic. I was touched and honored to celebrate his life with them.

Now for the pastoral perspective.

In my remarks at the funeral, I reminded everyone that Catholic social teaching reminds us that every person is entitled to be treated with dignity and respect. This dignity is intrinsic, following as it does from our being created in the image of God. For Catholics, the reflection of that dignity is seen in our participation in the sacramental life of the Church.

I know that the loved ones who gathered at that man's funeral were comforted by the words of the liturgy and the peace that the rites of the Church brings to members of a grieving community. I am convinced that to deny these rites on any basis, let alone to be as discriminatory in their administration as Bishop Paprocki's decree, is contrary to the example given us by Christ.

Christians around the world just celebrated three post-Easter Holy Days that ought to remind us of the fact that God's love is unconditionally given to all. At Pentecost, we gratefully acknowledged that the Spirit of the Lord is a gift bestowed upon all humans; at Holy Trinity, we joyfully recalled that the divine perichoresis is a continuous movement of all-embracing love; and at Corpus Christi, we rejoiced in the fact that the Eucharist unites us with one another and with God in bonds of joy and love. The great truths celebrated in these three Holy Days are basics of our faith. What God ordains cannot and should not be set aside by ecclesial decrees.

Consequently, we in the American National Catholic Church (ANCC) reject completely the idea that Holy Mother Church, founded from the blood and water flowing from the side of Christ, would ever deny her children the comfort and succor of Christ's presence in the sacramental life of the Church. Bishop Thomas Paprocki of Springfield's decree is, in essence, the antithesis of our experience of the Church.

Most Rev. George R. Lucey, FCM

Presiding Bishop

The American National Catholic Church

Discussion Questions

1. How do these letters interpret freedom of conscience as a theological rather than merely political principle?

2. In what ways do the texts demonstrate the development of doctrine while remaining rooted in tradition?

3. How does pastoral accompaniment function as a mode of moral theology in these letters?

4. What tensions emerge between institutional norms and lived human experience, and how are they addressed?

5. How do these letters reframe inclusion as an ecclesial conversion rather than a concession?

Chapter V: Liturgy and Sacraments (*Sacrosanctum Concilium*)

Introduction to the Letters in This Category

The pastoral letters in this final category address the Church's liturgical and sacramental life—the privileged place where theology is enacted rather than merely expressed. Grounded in *Sacrosanctum Concilium*, these texts reflect the Council's insistence that the liturgy is the source and summit of the Church's life and must be accessible, participatory, and pastorally responsive.

Questions of liturgical language, Eucharistic discipline, and sacramental practice are treated here not as technical rubrics but as matters of ecclesiology and pastoral care. The guiding principle throughout is the Council's call for full, conscious, and active participation by all the faithful. When sacramental practice becomes a tool of exclusion or ideological enforcement, it ceases to function as a sign of grace.

These letters reflect a sacramental theology influenced by postconciliar thinkers who emphasize encounter, symbol, and communal meaning over legalism. The Eucharist, in particular, is consistently presented not as a reward for moral perfection but as nourishment for a pilgrim people in need of grace.

As introductions to the letters that follow, these reflections invite the reader to approach ANCC liturgical practice as an expression of deeply Catholic faith—one that honors tradition while remaining attentive to the pastoral realities of the faithful. In doing so, they affirm the Council's vision of a liturgy that truly builds up the Body of Christ and sends it forth for the life of the world.

22 June 2021

Memorial of Ss. Thomas More and John Fisher

The Most Reverend George R. Lucey, FCM,
Presiding Bishop of the American National Catholic Church,
Responds to the USCCB on Communion

In the name of the Father, and of the + Son, and of the Holy Spirit!

Dear Sisters and Brothers in Christ:

At their annual June meeting, the United States (Roman) Catholic Conference of Bishops (USCCB) voted by nearly a 3-to-1 margin to draft a teaching document on receiving Communion.

The official USCCB rationale for the document is concern that only about one-third of practicing Roman Catholics in the United States believe in the Real Presence. This is genuinely worrisome, and I applaud the bishops desire to educate the faithful.

But the way in which they're going about doing so is disingenuous. Apparently, the unstated motivation behind the proposed document for at least some of the bishops is to deny communion to elected officials, President Biden in particular, who publicly support the 1973 Roe v Wade Supreme Court decision.

More than one observer has noted that this appears to be an alarming "weaponization" of the Holy Eucharist, a not-so-subtle warning to Roman Catholic "liberal" politicians and public figures. They point out that the USCCB wasn't nearly as forceful in responding to the personal and public moral lapses of the immediately previous administration.

In urging the bishops to refrain from this weaponization, Pope Francis reminded them that the Eucharist isn't a reward for saints but nourishment for sinners. I agree with this position.

Receiving the Body and Blood of the Lord changes our very mode of being because as the Vatican-II Council reminds us, it is "the source and summit of the Christian life." (Lumen Gentium 11) It serves to rejuvenate us spiritually by conforming us more closely to the image of God in which we're made. It binds the faithful together in genuine Christian koinonia. It strengthens the members Christ's Body to proclaim the Gospel and serve the world.

I appreciate that there are strong feelings on both sides of the abortion issue. But using the Eucharist as a weapon in the political debate is a sacrilege that inevitably will damage the Christian community. I'm confident that Christ at the Last Supper was very much aware of the sinners in his midst—including Judas Iscariot—when he instituted the Eucharist. Yet there is no evidence that he fed some and withheld from others. Instead, he welcomed everyone to the table. His Body and Blood are love gifts generously offered to us all.

We in the American National Catholic Church joyfully follow his example of profligate love. We welcome everyone, as the Lord did, to his table, and we pray that the USCCB bishops will do likewise.

Most Rev. George R. Lucey, FCM
Presiding Bishop
The American National Catholic Church

December 1, 2011

Pastoral Letter by The Most Reverend George R. Lucey, FCM Regarding Recent Liturgical Language Changes by the Roman Catholic Church

Grace and peace in the name of our Lord Jesus Christ!

We of the American National Catholic Church (ANCC) are aware of the recent changes in the sacred liturgy implemented by our Roman Catholic brothers and sisters on the First Sunday of Advent 2011. In the short time since the implementation, my office has received numerous inquires regarding our position on the liturgical change. I am using this opportunity to address this important matter.

As a national expression of the Catholic Church, we derive our Apostolic Succession and Catholic identity from Rome through Bishop Carlos Duarte-Costa of Brazil. Similar to Bishop Duarte-Costa, we found it necessary to proclaim the ancient truth of our Catholic faith apart from the jurisdiction of the Vatican.

We inherit a rich tradition. Bishop Duarte-Costa was a prophetic herald of the reforms of the Second Vatican Council. In as early as 1936, he called for the celebration of the liturgy in the vernacular while facing the people, a greater role of the laity in the liturgy including as Eucharistic ministers, and reception of the Eucharist in both bread and wine.

His foresight in founding the Apostolic Catholic Church of Brazil anticipated the liturgical reforms expressed in the Constitution on the Sacred Liturgy (*Sacrosantum Consilium*) solemnly promulgated by His Holiness Pope Paul VI and the bishops of the Second Vatican Council on December 4, 1963. With near unanimity, the College of Bishops supported the liturgical reforms by a vote of 2,147 in favor with only 4 bishops voting in opposition.

These reforms were translated into the New Order of the Mass (Novus Ordo) through the beautiful language enjoyed by Western Rite Roman Catholics for the past 45 years. The English translation was meticulously developed by the International Commission on English in the Liturgy (ICEL), approved by the United States Conference of Catholic Bishops with final approval by Pope Paul VI.

The celebration and remembrance of Christ's redemptive action in the liturgy is the central prayer of the Church. As so eloquently stated in the Dogmatic Constitution on the Church (*Lumen Gentium*), the Eucharist is both "the fount and apex of the whole Christian life." Full and active participation of the laity is a forgone conclusion.

Given its centrality in the life of the Church, the liturgy must be rooted in the language and cultural expression of the community. In particular, liturgical prayer must naturally grow out of the culture of the assembly, not handed down from another time or transliterated from an ancient language. Any language that is archaic, remote, or incomprehensible does not serve this purpose. We need to look no further than the writings of the Council itself. As stated in the Constitution on the Sacred Liturgy, paragraph #21:

> "Both text and rites should be drawn so that they express more clearly the holy things which they signify. The Christian people, as far as possible, should be able to understand them easily." (emphasis added)

And continuing in paragraph #34, we read that liturgical texts should:

> "*. . . be short, clear, and free from useless repetition.* They should be within the people's power of comprehension and normally should not require much attention." (emphasis added)

We of the ANCC carefully reviewed the proposed changes in the third edition of the Roman Missal and concluded that they did not reflect the Council's wisdom. For us, any change in the liturgical language must assure that the text is accessible and intelligible while remaining pastorally sensitive to the assembly.

All liturgical language must work for people of the third millennium. This includes children, teens and adults with varying degrees of education and those for whom English is a second language. Further, the use of male-dominated language is anachronistic, offending the sensitivities of many while diminishing the inclusion of the entire assembly.

Based on these standards, we found the proposed changes of the Roman Missal 3 wanting. Therefore, all ANCC liturgical celebrations will continue to follow the translation of the Roman Missal 2.

The ANCC remains dedicated to the full expression of the vision of the Second Vatican Council – a vision that remains unrealized. We see in the Council's call for liturgical reform, a greater invitation to participate in the communal prayer of the entire Church and a call to share more fully in the life of Christ.

It is our position that the liturgy of the New Order of the Mass (Novus Ordo) as translated in the Roman Missal 2 to be a more accurate expression of the all-inclusive love of God at the heart of the Catholic faith. We dedicate ourselves to preserving and continuing the reforms begun by the Holy Spirit at the Second Vatican Council.

Sincerely yours in Christ,

Most Reverend George R. Lucey, FCM
Presiding Bishop

Discussion Questions

1. How do these letters reflect Vatican II's emphasis on full, conscious, and active participation in the liturgy?

2. In what ways is Eucharistic theology linked to social responsibility and communion?

3. How do these texts resist both rigid legalism and liturgical relativism?

4. What pastoral criteria are used to evaluate liturgical language and sacramental discipline?

5. How does a sacramental worldview shape the ANCC's broader social and ecclesial vision?

Conclusion: Catholic Social Teaching in an ANCC Key — Communion, Conscience, and the Future of the Church

The pastoral letters gathered in this volume offer more than commentary on particular events or moments of crisis; taken together, they articulate a coherent ecclesial vision. They reveal how the American National Catholic Church understands itself as a Catholic Church formed by the Second Vatican Council and committed to receiving its teaching not as a historical artifact but as a living mandate.

Catholic Social Teaching, as these letters demonstrate, is not a parallel body of doctrine standing apart from the Church's sacramental life. It flows directly from the Church's understanding of the human person created in the image of God and redeemed in Christ. While its foundational principles remain constant, their application must always be discerned anew in light of historical realities (*Gaudium et Spes*, 26).

One of the most consistent threads running through these letters is the primacy of communion. Drawing deeply from *Lumen Gentium*, the ANCC understands the Church as a sacrament of unity—a people gathered by grace rather than uniformity. Authority, doctrine, and sacramentality are all ordered toward this end: the building up of the Body of Christ in love.

Equally central is the Council's teaching on conscience and religious freedom (Dignitatis Humanae). These letters affirm conscience not as a license for relativism, but as the privileged place where the human person encounters moral truth and responds to God's call. By emphasizing accompaniment and discernment, the ANCC remains firmly within Catholic moral tradition while resisting reductive or punitive approaches to ethical complexity.

Finally, these pastoral letters witness to a sacramental worldview that resists ideology. Catholic Social Teaching here is neither partisan nor abstract. It is Eucharistic in shape, pastoral in tone, and hopeful in orientation. In a time of polarization and fear, the ANCC offers a Catholicism confident enough to listen, courageous enough to speak, and humble enough to learn.

In this light, the American National Catholic Church offers not a departure from Catholic Social Teaching, but a particular and prayerful embodiment of it—one shaped by the Gospel, attentive to the world, and trusting in the Spirit who continues to guide the Church into all truth.

References

Congar, Yves. *True and False Reform in the Church*. Liturgical Press, 2011.

Francis. *Fratelli Tutti*. Vatican Press, 2020.

Second Vatican Council. "Dignitatis Humanae." *Vatican Council II: Constitutions, Decrees, Declarations*, Vatican Press, 1965.

Second Vatican Council. "Gaudium et Spes." *Vatican Council II: Constitutions, Decrees, Declarations*, Vatican Press, 1965.

Second Vatican Council. "Lumen Gentium." *Vatican Council II: Constitutions, Decrees, Declarations*, Vatican Press, 1964.

Appendix: Sample Syllabus

Graduate-Level Course Syllabus (10 Weeks)

Course Title

Peace as Communion: Vatican II, Catholic Social Teaching, and Pastoral Theology in Practice

Course Description

This graduate seminar examines Catholic Social Teaching through the pastoral letters of the American National Catholic Church, read in dialogue with the Second Vatican Council and contemporary Catholic theology. The course emphasizes ecclesial discernment, conscience, communion, and sacramentality as lived theological practices.

Course Objectives

By the end of the course, students will be able to:

- Articulate Vatican II's methodological approach to theology and social engagement
- Analyze pastoral letters as sources of lived Catholic moral theology
- Evaluate the relationship between doctrine, conscience, and pastoral practice
- Critically engage Catholic Social Teaching in contemporary contexts

Weekly Schedule

Week 1 – Vatican II as Hermeneutical Key

Readings: *Gaudium et Spes* §§1–11; Hermeneutical Key (Lucey)

Week 2 – The Church and the Modern World

Readings: ANCC letters on violence and racism; *Gaudium et Spes* §§26–32

Week 3 – Catholic Social Teaching as Living Tradition

Readings: *Populorum Progressio*; *Fratelli Tutti* (selected sections)

Week 4 – The Church as People of God

Readings: *Lumen Gentium* §§1–17; ANCC letters on ministry and vocation

Week 5 – Authority, Repentance, and Reform

Readings: ANCC letters on abuse and accountability; Congar, *True and False Reform*

Week 6 – Ecumenism and Catholic Identity

Readings: *Unitatis Redintegratio*; selected ANCC ecumenical correspondence

Week 7 – Conscience, Freedom, and Human Dignity

Readings: *Dignitatis Humanae*; ANCC letters on inclusion and conscience

Week 8 – Moral Theology, Accompaniment, and Development

Readings: Farley, *Just Love* (selected); Cahill, selected essays; ANCC texts

Week 9 – Liturgy, Sacrament, and Social Witness

Readings: *Sacrosanctum Concilium*; Chauvet, *Symbol and Sacrament* (selected)

Week 10 – Communion, Hope, and the Future of the Church

Readings: Conclusion chapter; student presentations

Course Requirements

- Active seminar participation (20%)
- Weekly reflection papers (30%)
- Final integrative paper or pastoral-theological project (50%)

Concluding Pedagogical Note

This course assumes that theology is not only studied but also practiced. Students are encouraged to read the pastoral letters prayerfully, critically, and in dialogue with their own ministerial or academic contexts.

Appendix: Canonical and Theological Clarification on Validity and Liceity

1. Introduction

The distinction between validity and licitness is foundational in Catholic sacramental theology and canon law. Because the American National Catholic Church (ANCC) is often described in terms of these categories, this appendix offers a precise and formal clarification of their meaning and their application to the ANCC's sacramental and ecclesial life. The purpose is not polemical, but explanatory—situating the ANCC within the broader Catholic theological tradition and articulating the basis upon which it understands its ministry as authentically Catholic.

2. Validity in Catholic Sacramental Theology

2.1 Definition

In Catholic theology, a sacrament is considered valid when it truly takes place—i.e., when it effects what the Church understands the sacrament to signify. Validity concerns the sacrament's ontological reality, not its canonical regularity.

A sacrament is valid when the essential elements are present:

- Proper matter
- Proper form
- Proper minister
- Proper intention

This framework is articulated in classical sacramental theology (Aquinas, ST III, q. 60–65) and reaffirmed in the 1983 Code of Canon Law (cc. 840–878).

2.2 Apostolic Succession and Holy Orders

For Holy Orders, validity requires:

- A bishop who has himself been validly ordained
- The laying on of hands
- The consecratory prayer

- The intention to ordain as the Church intends

The Roman Catholic Church holds that episcopal ordinations performed by bishops in valid apostolic succession—whether or not they are in juridical communion with Rome—are valid but illicit (cf. Apostolicae Curae; CIC c. 1012–1014; CDF doctrinal notes).

2.3 Application to the ANCC

The ANCC affirms that its episcopal lineage is part of the historic stream of apostolic succession recognized by the Catholic tradition. Therefore, according to the Church's own theological criteria, the sacraments celebrated by ANCC clergy—especially the Eucharist, Confirmation, Reconciliation, Anointing of the Sick, and Holy Orders—are valid.

This affirmation is theological, not juridical. It does not claim canonical recognition by the Roman Catholic Church, but simply acknowledges the sacramental reality as understood in Catholic theology.

3. Liceity in Canon Law

3.1 Definition

A sacrament is licit when it is celebrated in accord with the laws and disciplinary norms of the Church. Liceity concerns canonical regularity, not sacramental reality.

A sacrament may be:

- Valid and licit

- Valid but illicit

- Invalid and illicit

- Invalid but attempted

The Roman Catholic Church applies the category "illicit" to sacramental acts performed outside its juridical structures or without the required canonical mandate (CIC c. 1382; c. 1015).

3.2 Application to the ANCC

The ANCC acknowledges that, from the perspective of the Roman Catholic Church, its sacramental acts are considered illicit—that is, performed outside the canonical jurisdiction of Rome. The ANCC accepts this designation without dispute, recognizing that liceity is a matter of ecclesiastical law, not sacramental theology.

This acknowledgment does not diminish the ANCC's understanding of its sacramental life as valid, nor its self-understanding as authentically Catholic. Rather, it reflects a clear distinction between:

- Canonical jurisdiction (a matter of ecclesiastical governance)
- Sacramental validity (a matter of theology and apostolic continuity)

4. Ecclesial Communion and Catholic Identity

4.1 Catholicity Beyond Juridical Structures

Catholic tradition has long recognized that sacramental validity can exist outside full juridical communion. The Eastern Orthodox Churches, the Old Catholic Churches of the Union of Utrecht, and other apostolic bodies are examples of communities whose sacraments are regarded as valid despite imperfect communion with Rome.

This principle is articulated in Unitatis Redintegratio 15 and Lumen Gentium 8, which affirm that elements of sanctification and truth exist outside the visible boundaries of the Roman Catholic Church.

4.2 The ANCC's Self-Understanding

The ANCC situates itself within this broader theological landscape. It understands its sacramental life, episcopal ministry, and ecclesial governance as authentically Catholic, even while existing outside the canonical jurisdiction of Rome.

Its Catholic identity is grounded in:

- Apostolic succession
- Fidelity to the sacramental economy
- Reception of Vatican II
- Communion-oriented ecclesiology
- Pastoral governance ordered toward service and conscience

These are the same criteria by which the Catholic Church recognizes the authenticity of other apostolic communities.

5. Conclusion

The distinction between validity and licitness allows the ANCC to articulate its identity with clarity and humility:

- Valid, according to the Church's own sacramental theology

- Illicit, according to Roman Catholic canon law

Authentically Catholic, according to the criteria of apostolic faith, sacramental life, and conciliar ecclesiology

This appendix is offered not as a challenge to any ecclesial authority, but as a theological clarification. It reflects the ANCC's commitment to transparency, fidelity to the Catholic tradition, and service to the People of God.